The Holy Rosary, from the Writings
of the Fathers of the Church

The

Holy Rosary

From the Writings of the Fathers of the Church

F R .　　M A R K　　H I G G I N S

 CATHOLIC WAY PUBLISHING

Published in 2020 by Catholic Way Publishing.

Cover & Book design by Catholic Way Publishing.

This work is published for the greater glory of Jesus Christ through His most holy mother Mary and for the sanctification of the Church militant.

Ordering Information:

Orders by trade bookstores and wholesalers.

Please contact Ingram Content at www.ingramcontent.com.

ISBN-13: 978-1-78379-514-7 (PAPERBACK)

ISBN-13: 978-1-78379-515-4 (KINDLE E-BOOK)

ISBN-13: 978-1-78379-516-1 (EPUB E-BOOK)

10 9 8 7 6 5 4 3 2 1

Available in E-Book.

www.catholicwaypublishing.com

London, England, UK

2020

"Behold the handmaid of the Lord, be it done to me according to your word."

—THE BLESSED VIRGIN MARY, THE ANNUNCIATION

Contents

The Sorrowful Mysteries

39

The Glorious Mysteries

73

The Mysteries of Light

III

The Hopeful Mysteries

147

Introduction

WHEN OUR DIVINE LORD and Saviour Jesus Christ taught His saving Gospel to humanity during those precious years of His earthly ministry He taught and instructed the Blessed Apostles in far more truths than those contained in Sacred Scripture. How beautiful it is for a true son of the Catholic Church to hear those words, 'Sacred Tradition', what joy overflows from the heart of a true follower of Christ to know that the Word of God is contained not solely in Scripture, far from it, but overflows into Sacred Tradition. It is well known to all true Christians that Sacred Scripture refers to the Seventy Three books that are contained in the Holy Bible, books which are truly to be held as 'God breathed' and free from error. What however is Sacred Tradition? Sacred Tradition refers to all that was seen and heard by Our Divine Lord's audience and which was transmitted onwards through means other than through the inspired texts.

Sacred Tradition is not then found in its entirety in one concrete and identifiable location, but how could it be? It is far too immense to be contained in all the books in all the libraries of the world. The Church has infallibly identified for her children a number of monuments or mirrors of this Sacred Tradition, sources in which we do, with a certain degree of intensity, find the transmission of the saving revelation of Christ, completing that which is lacking in Sacred Scripture alone. Above all these monuments are the Councils and Creeds of the Early Church, her traditional liturgies and the writings of the Early Church Fathers.

When we pray the rosary, as Our Lady has explicitly requested that we do every day, we do well to meditate upon the actual scenes of the mysteries, to ponder those scenes and then to imitate the virtues exemplified therein. Many people will do this through reading passages of Scripture or indeed the writings of a saint, such as that of Blessed Anne Catherine Emmerich, the privileged seer of the events of salvation history.

In this short work I present before you another angle that you may wish to take, to pray the rosary through the lens of Sacred Tradition, to absorb the wisdom and insight from the Early Church, from the Fathers, from the liturgical texts and from other ancient writers who stood in such proximity to the very mouth of Christ. Primarily the rosary meditations are drawn, as the title of the book suggests, from the writings of the Fathers of the Church, men such as St. John Chrysostom, St. Basil the Great, St. Ephrem, St. Irenaeus, St. Bede and St. Bernard. I have, however, at times used the texts of other men, or of anonymous authors. My criteria in selecting these was always twofold, first, that they conform to teaching of the Catholic Church or secondly, where no definitive teaching has been established, that they conform to either the writings of Blessed Anne Catherine Emmerich or 'The Life of the Virgin Mary' by St. Maximus the Confessor', both of which fill in many hidden details of the Life of Our Saviour.

The usage of material from so called 'Apocryphal Gospels'

is thus explained, I have used them only when they accord with what we know to be true from reputable sources and where I have truly discerned that the information that they are conveying is worthy and profitable for meditation.

Indeed, it seems highly unfortunate that many early church texts have received this negative title when a large number of them, and ones used in this book, far from being Gnostic mythologies, were actually written by pious Catholic believers who intended to faithfully pass on something which they had heard, a tradition handed down to them concerning the lives of Our Blessed Lord and His Holy Mother.

In the case of Sacred Scripture every word is inspired, that is what marks it out uniquely from all other texts. The documents which contain elements of Sacred Tradition are not all so safeguarded, indeed, only those approved by the Magisterium in a specific manner such as the Nicene Creed can make an analogous claim of inerrancy. The Fathers of the Church, and more so the early writers who are not canonised, often share pieces of the Sacred Tradition but they will always do so with a potential admixture of error for they were writing as men without the guarantee of a continual safeguarding from error by the workings of the Holy Spirit. And so it must be said, some ideas or events proposed by the Fathers and early writers in the course of these meditations may or may not have taken place, there is an element of mystery, there is room for us all to ponder what they convey to us. But once again, let me reiterate, I have carefully selected passages which are in full accord with the Magisterium, and in areas that seemed to me novel or unusual I ensured that they conformed with either the revelations given to Blessed Anne Catherine Emmerich or "the Life of the Virgin "by Saint Maximus the Confessor before including them. A concrete case of this would be the meditation for the tenth bead of the Nativity, here I chose to convey an unusual tradition in one of the early writings, and yet it is a tradition that the privileged seer, Blessed Anne also received, and received independently of the text quoted which was hardly translated into any vernacular until the nineteenth century.

As with "The Holy Rosary through the visions of Blessed Anne Catherine Emmerich", a previous work of mine published by Catholic Way Publishing, I have included 'optional' mysteries for the Holy Rosary that readers may find useful. I have included these after the official fifteen mysteries, and these include the mysteries proposed by Pope John Paul II, 'The Mysteries of Light', and also a further set, 'The Hopeful Mysteries', based on the suggestion of Servant of God Frank Duff and a 'revelation' to someone close to the author.

As I close this introduction I close with a petition for prayer. Indeed, at this time in the history of the Church, I feel impelled to beg you all, in particular, to pray for the priests of the Holy Roman Catholic Church. Without priests, most certainly, we would all be damned, and yet those priests themselves, so many of them, tip toe along the edges of the very precipice of hell from which they would save us.

As you pray these beads then, my dear brothers and sisters in Christ, beg Our Lady's intercession for the clergy; for the bishops, the priests, the deacons, and indeed, most especially, for the Holy Father himself, which, at the time that this book was published was Pope Francis. Undoubtedly, at this time it is very manifest that evil has entered the Church. Surely this diabolic infiltration commenced with Judas, and it has continued ever since, but today it seems to have reached proportions perhaps only equivalent to the days of the Early Fathers, when wicked men like Arius, Nestorius and Valentinus sowed their diabolical doctrines and practices in the Christ's field, which is the Catholic Church. Perhaps, for this reason, the words of the Holy Fathers, which are shared in this simple book, will effect even more impact within our souls, for they wrote and prayed in times very much like ours, when many bishops had succumb to error, and the Lord Himself seemed to be silent, sleeping below deck, while the storm raged on above.

In the end, of course, her Immaculate Heart will triumph, Russia will be converted, and a period of peace will be given to the world. The Evil One has his hour, but God has His eternity. Until then, let us pray for priests, for most certainly, on the holiness of priests is balanced all things, and without this, only chastisement will befall us.

Yours, in the Immaculate Heart of Mary, Refuge of Sinners,
FATHER MARK HIGGINS

The Feast of Saint Raphael the Archangel, 2020
FRMARKHIGGINS@GMAIL.COM

NOTE ON PRAYING THE ROSARY USING THIS BOOK

If you are praying the rosary alone, it is suggested that you read the initial text before commencing the Our Father, afterwards the ten paragraphs of additional meditation could either be read before or during each Hail Mary. In a group setting a leader is required to read aloud each paragraph and commence each Hail Mary. The experience of the editor is that, in private use, with a prayerful silent reading of each passage, to say five mysteries will take at least 30 minutes and for some people closer to 45. If you feel the movements of grace pulling you into a simpler contemplation of a mystery as you read a paragraph, do not resist the Holy Spirit, and allow yourself to be at rest in the affect (the response of the heart) which Almighty God is stirring from within your soul.

In addition to the Fifteen Mysteries of the Holy Rosary, meditations are also included for those who wish to consider the mysteries proposed by Pope John Paul II, the Mysteries of Light, and, additionally a further set of mysteries prepared by the author, the Hopeful Mysteries. These further mysteries allow the reader to contemplate additional material offered to us by our visionary and cover events prior to the Joyful Mysteries, these are given as — The Creation of all things in Christ, the Promise of the Redeemer and Co-Redemptrix, the Birth of the Immaculate Virgin Mary, the Presentation of Mary as a girl in the Temple, and the Chaste Espousals of Mary and Joseph.

It is customary to commence the Holy Rosary with the Sign of the Cross, the Apostles Creed, and then, for the intentions of the Holy Father, an Our Father, a Hail Mary, and a Glory Be. After completing five mysteries we then say some concluding prayers centred around the Hail Holy Queen, these are contained at the end of this short work.

NOTE ON SOURCE MATERIAL

Almost the entirety of this work is drawn from the collections of the Fathers of the Church by Philip Schaff and Henry Wace, this includes those sources labelled "apocryphal". Their work is now in the public domain and has been used throughout this work. I have, at times, edited the material given. Universally I have made the language consistent with modern English both in grammar and spelling. Sometimes for sake of brevity or comprehensibility I have removed sentences or words from a given paragraph. In a few occasions I have made minor alterations to structure, or added a few words of context to, again, improve the clarity of a given passage or to ensure that some degree of flow is maintained between the ten beads of each mystery. For that reason I do not recommend using this book as a reference book for scholarly work on the Fathers of the Church, there are other books for that purpose, the purpose of this work is devotional rather than academic.

Additional Public Domain works have also been used in a small minority of instances, these include the translations of the ancient hymns of Byzantine and Syriac traditions.

One published work has been used. As you will see, I have used ten short quotes from the "The Life of the Virgin" by St. Maximus the Confessor, Translated by Stephen Shoemaker and published by Yale University Press. This work is an excellent and unparalleled account of the Life of the Virgin Mary, and I wholeheartedly recommend it to you as a companion to the writings of Blessed Anne Catherine Emmerich. All the short quotes from this work are referenced and placed in quotation marks to emphasise that I am quoting from a published source and without amending the quotation.

All images used in this book are works in the Public Domain available through Wikimedia Commons.

The Joyful Mysteries

The Annunciation

THE FRUIT OF THIS MYSTERY

Docility and obedience to the inspirations of the Guardian Angel

ET US LEARN FROM this Virgin how to bear ourselves, let us learn by her devout utterance, above all, let us learn by this holy mystery to be timid, to avoid any unnecessary company, and to shrink from human praise. Let all women learn from the example of modesty set here before us. The Virgin Mary, upon whom the stare of men had never been fixed was alone in her chamber, and was found only by an Angel. There was neither companion nor witness there, that what passed might not be debased in gossip, and the Angel saluted her. The message of God to the Virgin was a mystery so great that it cannot be uttered by the mouth of man, but by an Angel. For the first time on earth the words are spoken, "The Holy Spirit shall come upon you." The holy maiden hears and believes. Finally she replies, "Behold the handmaiden of the Lord; be it done to me according to your word." Here is an example of lowliness, here is a pattern of true devotion. At the very moment she is chosen to be the Mother of the Lord she declares herself to be His handmaid. The knowledge that she was chosen to this high vocation brought about in Mary only an act of humility. (ST. AMBROSE)

OUR FATHER   Our Father, Who art in Heaven, hallowed be Thy name, Thy kingdom come, Thy will be done, on earth as it is in heaven. Give us this day our daily bread; and forgive us our trespasses, as we forgive those who trespass against us; and lead us not into temptation, but deliver us from evil. Amen.

HAIL MARY (10)   Hail Mary, Full of Grace, the Lord is with thee. Blessed art thou among women and blessed is the fruit of thy womb, Jesus. Holy Mary, Mother of God, pray for us sinners now, and at the hour of our death. Amen.

1. The Archangel Gabriel received his commandments from the Lord, it was as if he was told, "Go, O Angel, for sin has soiled my creation, and has darkened where I created beauty. I am going to have mercy on him who was attacked, and I wish to make war with him who fought against him. I wish for all of the heavenly powers to know, but to you alone I impart the mystery. Go to the Virgin Mary, go to the Spiritual Gate

of which the Prophet said, 'Glorious things have been said of you, O City of God.' Go to My Paradise. Go to the Eastern City. Go to her who is the worthy dwelling-place of the Word. Go to the second Heaven on earth. Tell her of My coming. Go to her who is My prepared holy place. Go to the Bridal Chamber of My incarnation. Go to the pure Bridal Chamber of My nativity in the flesh. Speak to the ears of this rational Ark. But do not be fearsome, do not trouble the soul of the Virgin, instead, first cry out to her with a voice of joy, and say to her, 'Hail, O Full of grace'". (ST. JOHN CHRYSOSTOM)

2. The Father in His mercy beckoned to His Eternal Son to descend and to redeem that which He had once fashioned, and to Gabriel the angel did He instruct to prepare the path before His descent. With David's daughter did His mercy shine out, for she was to be mother of Him Who had given birth to Adam and to the whole world, and Whose name is older than the sun. And so that Divine Will which cannot be grasped summoned the angel, sending him out from the angelic hosts on a mission to bring the glad news to a pure virgin. A letter did he bring that had been sealed with the mystery which from all ages had been hidden; He filled it with greeting to the young girl and fair hope for all the worlds. "O blessed of women" he said, "in you it has pleased the Most High to dwell; have no fear, for in you has Grace bent down to pour mercy upon the world. It is the Father's love that has so willed that in your virginity you should give birth to the Son. O child, give thanks to Him Who has held you worthy to be His mother having Him as your son." (SIXTH CENTURY, SYRIAC DIALOGUE HYMN)

3. The Virgin took the pitcher and went out to fill it with water. And, behold, a voice called to her saying, "Hail, you who have received grace, the Lord is with you, blessed are you among women!", and she looked round on the right hand and on the left to see where the voice had come from. The Virgin went away, trembling, to her house, and put down the pitcher; and taking up the purple wool to spin, she sat down on her seat, and drew it out. And, behold, an angel of the Lord stood before her, saying, "Fear not, Mary; for you have found grace before the Lord of all, and you shall conceive, according to His word." (SECOND CENTURY, THE PROTOEVANGELIUM OF JAMES)

4. You have learned, O Virgin, things which had been kept concealed till now from even the angels. You have heard, O purest one, things of which even the choir of inspired men was never deemed worthy. Moses, David, Isaiah and Daniel, and all the prophets prophesied of Him; but the manner of their fulfilment, they did not know. Yet you alone, O purest Virgin, are now made the recipient of things of which all these were kept in ignorance, even more, the fulfilment of most of these wonders has depended on you. (ST. GREGORY THAUMATURGUS)

5. Hail, O full of grace! Hail, O highly favoured, O ever-blooming vine that makes glad the souls of those who honour you! Hail, O highly favoured! O soil that bears bounteous fruit, for you have brought forth in accordance with the law of nature, or rather, above nature, by reason that God the Word from above has taken His abode in you, and formed the new Adam in your holy womb through the power of the Holy Spirit. The reality of His body was assumed from her

body. And just as the pearl comes of the two natures, namely lightning and water, so also our Divine Lord Jesus Christ proceeds, without fusion and without mutation, from the pure, chaste, undefiled, holy Virgin Mary. He is perfect in divinity and perfect in humanity, in all things equal to the Father, and in all things consubstantial with us, apart from sin. (ST. GREGORY THAUMATURGUS)

6. "But consider the wisdom of the blessed and all-holy Virgin and her excessive love of virginity. She believed the archangel's message but was astonished by the matter. That is why she answered and said, "How can this be, for I have not known a man, nor is this possible, because I have been consecrated immaculately to God, and without a man conception is not possible." For this was her fear and distress, that he related the loss of her virginity, which was steadfast in her heart, to remain in virginity until she died." * (ST. MAXIMUS THE CONFESSOR)

7. You have heard, O Virgin, that you will conceive and bear a son, you have heard that it will not be by man but by the Holy Spirit. The angel awaits an answer, it is time for him to return to God Who sent him. We too are waiting, O Lady, for your word of compassion, the sentence of condemnation weighs heavily upon us. The price of our salvation is offered to you. We shall be set free at once if you consent. Tearful Adam with his sorrowing family begs this of you, O loving Virgin, in their exile from Paradise. Abraham begs it, David begs it. All the other holy patriarchs, your ancestors, ask it

---

* Maximus the Confessor, *"The Life of the Virgin"*, (Yale: Bloomsbury 2012), 59.

of you, as they dwell in the country of the shadow of death. This is what the whole earth waits for, prostrate at your feet. It is right in doing so, for on your word depends comfort for the wretched, ransom for the captive, freedom for the condemned, indeed, salvation for all the sons of Adam, the whole of your race. (ST. BERNARD)

8. Answer quickly, O Virgin. Reply in haste to the angel, or rather through the angel to the Lord. Answer with a word, receive the Word of God. Speak your own word, conceive the Divine Word. Breathe a passing word, embrace the Eternal Word. Why do you delay, why are you afraid? Believe, give praise and receive. Let humility be bold, let modesty be confident. Though modest silence is pleasing, dutiful speech is now more necessary. Open your heart to faith, O blessed Virgin, your lips to praise, your womb to the Creator. See, the desired of all nations is at your door, knocking to enter. Arise, hasten, open. Arise in faith, hasten in devotion, open in praise and thanksgiving. "Behold the handmaid of the Lord", she says, "be it done to me according to your word." (ST. BERNARD)

9. "O angel", replied the maiden, "reveal to me why it has pleased your Lord to dwell in a mere poor girl. The world is full of kings' daughters, so why does He want me, who am totally destitute?" The angel responded, "It would have been easy for Him to dwell in a rich girl, but it is with your poverty that He has fallen in love, so that He may become one with the poor and enrich them when He has been revealed." "In that case, O angel", replied the Virgin, "I will not answer back. If the Holy Spirit shall come to me, I am His maidservant

and He has authority; let it be to me, Lord, in accordance with Your word." (SIXTH CENTURY, SYRIAC DIALOGUE HYMN)

10. O womb of Mary in which was conceived the living heaven, wider than the wideness of the heavens. This heaven is clearly much more divine and awesome than the first. Indeed, He Who created the sun in the first heaven would Himself be born of this second heaven, as the Sun of Justice. Mary, surpassing the Cherubim, exalted beyond the Seraphim, is placed near to God. (ST. JOHN DAMASCENE)

GLORY BE TO THE FATHER   Glory be to the Father, and to the Son, and to the Holy Spirit, as it was in the beginning, is now and ever shall be, world without end. Amen.

THE FATIMA PRAYER   O my Jesus, forgive us our sins, save us from the fires of hell, lead all souls to heaven, especially those in most need of Thy mercy.

The Visitation

THE FRUIT OF THIS MYSTERY

An increase in humility, especially when performing works of mercy

"AND HOW IS IT that the Mother of my Lord comes to me?", It is not ignorance that makes Elizabeth say this, she knows well that grace is at work and that Mary has come to her through the impulse of the Holy Spirit, but here she is recognising that the visit is not from human merit but a gift of grace, and so she says, "How is it given to me?", that is to say, "What happiness is this that the

Mother of my Lord comes to me? I admit to being completely unworthy. How is it given to me? By what justice, what actions, for what merits?" These are not merely customary words between women, Elizabeth senses the miracle, she recognises the mystery, the Mother of the Lord is fruitful of the Word, full of God. (ST. AMBROSE)

OUR FATHER   Our Father, Who art in Heaven, hallowed be Thy name, Thy kingdom come, Thy will be done, on earth as it is in heaven. Give us this day our daily bread; and forgive us our trespasses, as we forgive those who trespass against us; and lead us not into temptation, but deliver us from evil. Amen.

HAIL MARY (10)   Hail Mary, Full of Grace, the Lord is with thee. Blessed art thou among women and blessed is the fruit of thy womb, Jesus. Holy Mary, Mother of God, pray for us sinners now, and at the hour of our death. Amen.

1. When the feast came round for Zechariah to enter before the Lord to fulfil his service by offering incense on the altar and partaking of atonement, he beheld an angel of the Lord on the right of the altar of incense, and he trembled in fear of him. The spiritual being approached, reassuring him with gentle and humble speech, saying, "Fear not, Zechariah, the Lord is pleased with your prayer and has sent me to give you good tidings, you and Elizabeth your wife have done well before the Lord; and now she is pregnant and will bear you a child in whom you and many will rejoice. While still in the womb the Lord will fill him with the Holy Spirit and consecrate him." But Zechariah doubted at his presence and did not believe the message, replying, "How sir shall this be, that Elizabeth should have a child. She is old, and barren too;

and I am old, as you can see. However much you speak trying to persuade me, your words will not convince me." The Angel answered, "Look at Abraham from whom you descended, he was an old man, and his wife was barren as well, yet she gave birth. I wish you had never questioned it, Zechariah, you really should have believed me; Isaiah prophesied about your son long ago, as he was instructed. until Elizabeth gives birth your mouth shall be bound, without speech, and so will the gates of your ears, unable to hear." When it became apparent to the Hebrews what had occurred, astonishment reigned among them, their minds were occupied with the affair. They were amazed and full of wonder as they spoke to one another, saying, "What sort of son will this be, when all this takes place at his conception?" (FIFTH CENTURY, SYRIAC DIALOGUE HYMN)

2. As soon as Mary had learned of the maternity of the old and sterile woman, not because of a lack of faith in the prophecy, nor out of uncertainty of this announcement, nor out of doubt about the precedent provided, but in the joy of her desire to fulfil a pious duty, in the eagerness of joy, she went to the mountains. From now on, filled with God, how could she not rise hastily to the heights? Slow calculations are foreign to the grace of the Holy Spirit. Towards the heights the Virgin hastens, the Virgin who thinks to serve and forgets her pain, whose charity is her strength, overcoming her girlish delicacy, she leaves her house and goes. (ST. AMBROSE)

3. You have learned, virgins, the delicacy of Mary, learn her humility. She comes as a relative to her relative, as a younger to her elder, and not only does she come, but she is the first to salute. It is fitting that she knows how to honour her elders,

that she is both mistress of humility and perfect in modesty. It must indeed be remarked that the superior comes to help the inferior: Mary to Elizabeth and Christ to John. (ST. AMBROSE)

4. And Mary, with great joy, went away to the house of Elizabeth her kinswoman, and knocked at the door. When Elizabeth heard her, she threw down her needlework, ran to the door, and opened it. Seeing Mary she praised her, and said, "Why am I so honoured that the mother of my Lord should come to me? For, behold, that which is in me leapt in praise of your coming." But Mary gazed up into heaven, and said, "Who am I, O Lord, that all the generations of the earth should bless me?" And she remained three months with Elizabeth; and day by day she grew bigger. And Mary being afraid, went away to her own house, and hid herself from the sons of Israel. And she was sixteen years old when these mysteries happened. (SECOND CENTURY, THE PROTOEVANGELIUM OF JAMES)

5. Elizabeth first heard the voice, but John was the first to feel grace, Elizabeth perceived the arrival of Mary, John, that of the Lord, the woman that of the woman, the child that of the child. And, by a double miracle, the mothers prophesy under the inspiration of their children. The child shuddered, the mother was filled, the mother was not filled before her son, but the son, once filled with the Holy Spirit, also filled his mother. (ST. AMBROSE)

6. Although St. John the Baptist had not been born, already he prophesies and, while still in the enclosure of his mother's womb, confesses the coming of Christ with movements of joy since he couldn't do so with his voice. In this regard I think that the prophetic phrase is appropriate that says, "Before I

formed you in the womb I knew you, and before you were born I consecrated you." We ought not to marvel that after he was put in prison by Herod, from his confinement he continued to announce Christ to his disciples, when even confined in the womb he preached the same Lord by his movements. (ST. MAXIMUS OF TURIN)

7. May all of you have the soul of Mary to glorify the Lord, May the spirit of Mary live in each one of you to exult in God. If there is physically only a single Mother of Christ, by faith Christ is the fruit of all. Every soul, therefore, who achieves the state of grace magnifies the Lord, as the soul of Mary magnified the Lord, and as her spirit shuddered in the Saviour God. The soul that does right and religious work magnifies this image of God, in Whose likeness she was created. And in magnifying Him, she participates in His grandeur to a certain extent and finds herself elevated in it, she seems to reproduce His image in herself by the brilliant colours of her good works. (ST. AMBROSE)

8. Rachel cried to her husband, and said, "Give me sons." Blessed be Mary, in whose womb, although she did not ask, You chose to dwell in a most holy manner, O Gift that poured Itself upon her who received It. Hannah with bitter tears asked for a child, Sarah and Rebecca with vows and words, Elizabeth too with her prayer after having vexed herself for a long time, and yet all these eventually obtained their requests. Blessed be Mary, who without such vows and petitions, in her Virginity conceived and brought forth the Lord of all. Who else lulled a son in her bosom as Mary did? who ever dared to call her son, The Son of the Maker, Son of the Creator,

Son of the Most High? Who ever dared to speak to her son as one speaks to God in prayer? (ST. EPHREM)

9. Elizabeth marvelled that so great a person should come to see her and she asked, "How have I deserved to be thus visited by the mother of my Lord?", and in praise of her faith she said, "You are blessed for believing the things of God." This was high praise indeed, but Mary's utter humility would not allow her to keep anything for herself, it only made her the more eager to refer all the credit to God, for it was His blessings that were being praised in her. "You magnify me," the Virgin might have said, "because I am the Lord's mother, but my soul magnifies the Lord Himself. You say that your child leapt for joy when he heard my voice, but my spirit has found joy in God, Who is my Saviour, and your son too rejoices at hearing the bridegroom's voice, for he is the bridegroom's friend. You call me blessed because I have believed, but the reason why I have believed and am blessed is that the merciful God has looked down upon me from on high. If all generations are to count me blessed, it is because God has looked graciously upon His poor and lowly handmaid." (ST. BERNARD)

10. And Mary was in her sixth month; and, behold, Joseph came back from his work, and, entering into his house, he noticed that Mary was pregnant. And he hid his face, and threw himself on the ground upon the sackcloth, and wept bitterly. Joseph was greatly afraid, and retired from Mary, considering what he should do in regard to her. Joseph said to himself, "If I conceal her sin I find myself fighting against the law of the Lord; and if I expose her to the sons of Israel, I am afraid lest that which is in her be from an angel, and I

shall be found giving up innocent blood to the doom of death. What then shall I do with her? I will put her away from myself secretly." And night came upon him, and, behold, an angel of the Lord appeared to him in a dream, saying, "Do not fear for this maiden, for that which is in her is of the Holy Spirit; and she will bring forth a Son, and you shall call His name Jesus, for He will save His people from their sins." And Joseph arose from sleep, and glorified the God of Israel, Who had given him this grace, and he kept Mary in his home. (SECOND CENTURY, THE PROTOEVANGELIUM OF JAMES)

GLORY BE TO THE FATHER   Glory be to the Father, and to the Son, and to the Holy Spirit, as it was in the beginning, is now and ever shall be, world without end. Amen.

THE FATIMA PRAYER   O my Jesus, forgive us our sins, save us from the fires of hell, lead all souls to heaven, especially those in most need of Thy mercy.

The Nativity

THE FRUIT OF THIS MYSTERY

*Imitation of Christ in His spiritual poverty, His sovereign detachment
from earthly glories, and His love of remaining hidden from the
sinful, curious eye but manifest to those Who love Him*

THE SIGN GIVEN OF the Saviour's birth is not a child
enfolded in royal purple, but one wrapped with
rough pieces of cloth. He is not to be found in an
ornate golden bed, but in a manger. The meaning of this is
that He did not merely take upon Himself our lowly mortality,

but for our sakes took upon Himself the clothing of the poor. Though He was rich, yet for our sake He became poor, so that by His poverty we might become rich. Though He was Lord of heaven, He became a poor man on earth, to teach those who lived on earth that by poverty of spirit they might win the Kingdom of Heaven. (ST. BEDE)

OUR FATHER   Our Father, Who art in Heaven, hallowed be Thy name, Thy kingdom come, Thy will be done, on earth as it is in heaven. Give us this day our daily bread; and forgive us our trespasses, as we forgive those who trespass against us; and lead us not into temptation, but deliver us from evil. Amen.

HAIL MARY (10)   Hail Mary, Full of Grace, the Lord is with thee. Blessed art thou among women and blessed is the fruit of thy womb, Jesus. Holy Mary, Mother of God, pray for us sinners now, and at the hour of our death. Amen.

1. On that night, peace reigned over the whole Roman Empire in fulfilment of the song of the angels which declared 'peace on earth'. A fountain miraculously gushed forth in the cave of the nativity and the idols in Egypt and other places were thrown down. In Rome, a temple collapsed which had been built by Romulus and dedicated to a god of war, it had been a place where the demons used to gather and give oracles. On the night of the Saviour's birth they fled forth, crying, "We must depart for a virgin has brought forth without ceasing to be a virgin." (FRAGMENTS FROM OROSIUS, POPE INNOCENT I, ST. BEDE AND ST. IGNATIUS OF ANTIOCH)

2. The Virgin laid Him in the manger, and the God Who found man reduced to the level of the beasts is placed like

food in a manger, that we, having left behind our bestial life, might mount up to that degree of intelligence which befits man's nature, and whereas we had once been brutish in soul, now, by approaching the manger, even His own table, we find no longer fodder, but the Bread from Heaven, which is the Body of Life. (ST. CYRIL OF ALEXANDRIA)

3. And Joseph said to the midwife, "Come and see." And the midwife went away with him. And they stood before the cave, and behold a luminous cloud came and overshadowed it. A great light shone in the cave, and their eyes could not bear it, but after a few moments the light gradually decreased, until the infant appeared, who stretching upwards, desired to be fed by His mother. And the midwife cried out, and said, "This is a great day to me, because I have seen this strange sight, a virgin has brought forth, a wonder beyond the power of nature." (SECOND CENTURY, THE PROTOEVANGELIUM OF JAMES)

4. The Lord is born on earth, and He does not have even a cell in which to be born, for there was no room for Him in the inn. The entire human race had a place, and the Lord about to be born on earth had none. He found no room among men. He found no room in Plato, none in Aristotle, but in a manger, among beasts of burden and brute animals, and among the simple and the innocent. For that reason the Lord says in the Gospel, "The foxes have dens, and the birds of the air have nests, but the Son of Man has nowhere to lay His head." (ST. JEROME)

5. Surely if He had so willed it, He might have come moving the heavens, making the earth to shake and shooting forth His

thunderbolts, but such was not the way of His going forth. His desire was not to destroy, but to save, and to trample upon human pride from its very birth. For that reason, He is not only a man, but a poor man, and has chosen a poor mother, who had not even a cradle where she might lay her new born Child, as it follows, "And she laid Him in a manger." (ST. JOHN CHRYSOSTOM)

6. In the manger set apart for brute beasts did the Word of God repose, in order that He might impart to men, made irrational through sinful choice, the teachings of true reason. In the trough from which cattle eat was laid the heavenly Bread, in order that He might provide a spiritual sustenance to men who have come to live like animals. Angelic choirs encircled Him, singing of glory in heaven and of peace on earth. In heaven He was seated at the right hand of the Father, and in the manger He rested, as it were, upon the Cherubim. Yes, the manger was His cherubic throne, there was His royal seat. All holy, alone glorious upon the earth, holier than the holy of holies was that place where Christ our God rested. (ST. GREGORY THAUMATURGUS)

7. When Augustus' reigned alone upon earth, the many kingdoms of men came to end, and when You were made man of the pure Virgin, the many gods of idolatry were destroyed. The cities of the world passed under one single rule and the nations came to believe in one sovereign Godhead. The peoples were enrolled by the decree of Caesar, and we, the faithful, were enrolled in the Name of the Godhead, when You, our God, were made man. Great is Your mercy, all glory be to You. (ST. CASSIA)

8. But, as every one praises most what is within his reach, let us pass now to the cave which sheltered Christ and Mary. With what expressions and what language can we set before you the birthplace of the Saviour? The stall where He cried as a babe can be best honoured by silence; for words are inadequate to speak its praise. Where are the spacious porticoes? Where are the gilded ceilings? Where are the mansions furnished by the miserable toil of workers? Where are the costly halls raised for man's vile body to walk in? Where are the roofs that intercept the sky, as if anything could be finer than the expanse of heaven? Behold, in this poor crevice of the earth the Creator of the Heavens was born, here He was wrapped in swaddling clothes, here He was seen by the shepherds, here He was pointed out by the star, here He was adored by the wise men. This spot is holier, I would say, than any other shrine. (ST. JEROME)

9. And now let us consider the glory which accompanies the birth, the wailing and the cradle. He that is born is God with us. An Angel brings to the shepherds the news that Christ the Lord is born, the Saviour of the World. The light of a new star shines forth for the Magi, a heavenly sign escorts the Lord of Heaven. The Magi come and worship Him wrapped in swaddling clothes. After lives devoted to mystic rites of vain philosophy they bend their knees before a babe laid in His cradle. The inward reality is widely different from the outward appearance, their eyes see one thing, their souls another. An infant wails, angels are heard in praise. The baby wears coarse swaddling clothes and they worship Him as God. (ST. JOHN DAMASCENE)

10. Joseph was warned of Herod's plans in his sleep by the angel of the Lord, who said to him, "Take Mary and the child, and go into Egypt by the way of the desert." And so they went, according to the words of the angel. And as they journeyed, they were accompanied in the desert by lions and panthers. Wherever Joseph and the blessed Mary went, the fierce creatures went before them showing them the way, bowing their heads; they showed their submission by wagging their tails, and they adored the child with great reverence. And so the Holy Family walked among wolves and feared nothing, no one was harmed. They had with them two oxen drawing a waggon with provision for the journey, as well as some sheep. The lions directed them in their path and they did not hurt a single one of them, though they kept beside them. Then was fulfilled that which was spoken by the prophet, "The wolves shall feed with lambs, the lion and the ox shall eat straw together." (FOURTH CENTURY, INFANCY OF PSEUDO MATTHEW)

GLORY BE TO THE FATHER   Glory be to the Father, and to the Son, and to the Holy Spirit, as it was in the beginning, is now and ever shall be, world without end. Amen.

THE FATIMA PRAYER   O my Jesus, forgive us our sins, save us from the fires of hell, lead all souls to heaven, especially those in most need of Thy mercy.

The Presentation in the Temple

THE FRUIT OF THIS MYSTERY

A willingness to leave this short passing life at the summons of the Lord, whenever and however it may come

THE VIRGIN MARY, GOD's Blessed Mother, was, along with the son she bore, most free from all subjection to this requirement of the Jewish law, for she gave birth as a virgin. There is nothing in the law that would require such a woman to be cleansed by a saving sacrificial offering. But as Our Lord and Saviour, Who in His divinity was the

One Who gave the law, when He appeared as a human being, willed to be under the law, so too His blessed mother, who by a singular privilege was above the law, did not shun being made subject to the principles of the law. She did this for the sake of showing us an example of humility. (ST. BEDE)

OUR FATHER   Our Father, Who art in Heaven, hallowed be Thy name, Thy kingdom come, Thy will be done, on earth as it is in heaven. Give us this day our daily bread; and forgive us our trespasses, as we forgive those who trespass against us; and lead us not into temptation, but deliver us from evil. Amen.

HAIL MARY (10)   Hail Mary, Full of Grace, the Lord is with thee. Blessed art thou among women and blessed is the fruit of thy womb, Jesus. Holy Mary, Mother of God, pray for us sinners now, and at the hour of our death. Amen.

1. All the tribes of the people mourned and lamented at the death of the former priest, Zechariah, for three days and three nights. And after the three days, the priests consulted as to whom they should put in his place, and the lot fell upon Simeon. For it was he who had been warned by the Holy Spirit that he should not see death until he should see the Christ in the flesh. (SECOND CENTURY, THE PROTOE-VANGELIUM OF JAMES)

2. How many have gone astray by not understanding the mystery of Our Lord's nativity. The statement, "He Who opens the womb shall be called holy to the Lord" is more applicable to the special nativity of the Saviour than to any other birth, for Christ alone opened the closed doors of the womb of virginity, which nevertheless remained permanently

closed. This is the closed east gate, through which only the high priest enters and leaves, and nevertheless always remains closed. (ST. JEROME)

3. The just Simeon saw Christ with his eyes when he took the infant into his arms, but he also saw with his heart because he recognised the infant as the Son of God. Seeing Him in both ways, recognising the Son of God, and cuddling the One begotten of the Virgin, he said, "Now, Lord, You are letting Your servant go in peace, since my eyes have seen Your salvation." Notice what he said, he was being kept alive until he should see with his eyes the One he already perceived with faith. He took the baby, he cradled Him in his arms. On seeing the body, that is, on perceiving the Lord in the flesh, he said, "My eyes have seen Your salvation." (ST. AUGUSTINE)

4. Observe then that this just man, confined as it were in the prison house of his earthly frame, is longing to be loosed, that he may again be with Christ. Let whosoever would wish to be cleansed come into the temple, into Jerusalem, let him wait for the Lord's Christ, let him receive the Word of God, and embrace It as it were with the arms of his faith. Then let him depart that he might not see death, who has seen Life. (ST. AMBROSE)

5. But inasmuch as Simeon endured to carry in his weak arms that Majesty which the whole creation could not endure, it is evident that his weakness was made strong by the strength which he carried. Simeon, along with the whole of creation, was secretly upheld by the almighty strength of the Son. What a marvel! It looked as if Simeon was carrying Him who was sustaining him and all other creatures. His Majesty stooped

to our littleness. And now, how our hearts should be raised up from all other desires in order to reach Him. (ST. EPHREM)

6. If we marvel to hear that a woman was healed by touching the hem of His garment, what must we think of Simeon, who received the Infant Jesus in his arms, and rejoiced seeing that the little One he carried was He Who had come to let loose the captive! Knowing that no one could release him from the chains of the body with the hope of future life, but He Whom he held in his arms. Therefore it is said, "And he blessed God, saying, 'Lord, now let Your servant depart'", it was as if he was saying, "Until I held Christ I was in prison, only then could I escape from my bonds." (ORIGEN)

7. This blessed one, Mary, who had been found worthy of gifts surpassing nature, did at the time of the passion suffer the pangs which she had escaped at childbirth. When she saw Him put to death as a criminal, the man she knew to be God, her heart was torn through maternal compassion, and she was rent as if by a sword. This is the meaning of "and a sword will pierce through your own soul too". (ST. JOHN DAMASCENE)

8. The martyrdom of the Virgin is both set forth in the prophecy of Simeon and in the actual story of our Lord's passion. The holy old man said of the infant Jesus, "He has been established as a sign which will be contradicted." He went on to say to Mary, "And your own heart will be pierced by a sword." Truly, O blessed Mother, a sword has pierced your heart. Indeed, after your son gave up His life, the cruel spear, which was not withheld from His lifeless body, tore open His side. Clearly it did not touch His soul and could not harm Him, but it pierced your heart. For surely His soul

was no longer there, but yours could not be torn away. Thus the violence of sorrow cut through your heart, and we rightly call you more than a martyr, for indeed, your sharing in His suffering went beyond the endurance of physical suffering. She died in spirit through a love unlike any other since His. (ST. BERNARD)

9. It was not by chance that the Holy Spirit dwelt in the prophetess Anna. For the highest blessing, if any can possess it, is the grace of virginity, but if this cannot be, and then it passes to a woman to lose her husband, let her remain a widow. Indeed, not only after the death of her husband, but even while he is still living, the desire of widowhood ought to be in her mind, and if it fails to happen, her will and determination to be a widow might yet be crowned by the Lord. Her words should be, "This I vow and promise, that if a certain condition of life comes to be mine, I will do nothing else but remain inviolate and a widow." Most justly then was this holy woman, Anna, thought worthy to receive the gift of prophecy, because by long chastity and long fasting she had ascended to the height of virtue, as it follows, "She departed not from the temple but stayed there, night and day, with fasting and prayers." (ORIGEN)

10. The Mother of God, the most pure Virgin, carried the true light in her arms and brought Him to those who lay in darkness. Let all of us share in its splendour, and be so filled with it that no one remains in the darkness. Let us go together to meet and to receive with the aged Simeon the light Whose brilliance is eternal. Rejoicing with Simeon, let us sing a hymn of thanksgiving to God, the Father of Light, Who sent the True Light to dispel the darkness and to give us all a share in

His splendour. Through Simeon's eyes we too have seen the salvation of God which He prepared for all the nations and revealed as the glory of the new Israel, which is ourselves. As Simeon was released from the bonds of this life when he had seen Christ, so we too were at once freed from our old state of sinfulness. (ST. SOPHRONIUS)

GLORY BE TO THE FATHER   Glory be to the Father, and to the Son, and to the Holy Spirit, as it was in the beginning, is now and ever shall be, world without end. Amen.

THE FATIMA PRAYER   O my Jesus, forgive us our sins, save us from the fires of hell, lead all souls to heaven, especially those in most need of Thy mercy.

The Finding of the Boy Jesus in the Temple

THE FRUIT OF THIS MYSTERY

The strength and perseverance to find the life of grace, which is given to us by Our Saviour through His Catholic Church

HAVE YOU NOT READ in the Gospel the example of obedience set by the boy Jesus for the imitation of all other youths who aspire after holiness? For although He had remained behind in Jerusalem, and declared that it was necessary for Him to be about His Father's business, when His parents found Him, and would not consent to Him staying any longer, He did not disdain to follow them to Nazareth. The Master obeyed His disciples, God obeyed man, the Word, the Wisdom of the Father obeyed a poor artisan and his consort! And that is not all, the inspired narrative goes on to say, "and He was subject to them". (ST. BERNARD)

OUR FATHER   Our Father, Who art in Heaven, hallowed be Thy name, Thy kingdom come, Thy will be done, on earth as it is in heaven. Give us this day our daily bread; and forgive us our trespasses, as we forgive those who trespass against us; and lead us not into temptation, but deliver us from evil. Amen.

HAIL MARY (10)   Hail Mary, Full of Grace, the Lord is with thee. Blessed art thou among women and blessed is the fruit of thy womb, Jesus. Holy Mary, Mother of God, pray for us sinners now, and at the hour of our death. Amen.

1. The fact that the Lord came up every year to Jerusalem at the Passover shows His humility as a man, for it is a human obligation to gather collectively and offer sacrifices to God, conciliating Him with prayers. Accordingly the Lord, as a man, did among men what God by angels commanded men to do. Let us then follow the pattern of His mortal life, and thereby come to delight in beholding the glory of His divine nature. (ST. BEDE)

2. Once the feast had been celebrated, while the rest returned, Jesus secretly stayed behind. It is said, "when the days were accomplished", because the feast lasted seven days. But the reason of His remaining behind in secret was that His parents

might not be a hindrance to Him carrying on the discussion
with the lawyers, or perhaps to avoid appearing in some way
disrespectful to His parents. He therefore remains secretly, that
He might neither be kept away nor be considered disobedient.
(TENTH CENTURY, 'THE GREEK EXPOSITOR')

3. But someone will ask, how was it that the Son of God,
brought up by His parents with such care, could be left behind
from forgetfulness? To which it is answered, that the custom
of the children of Israel while assembling at Jerusalem on the
feast days, or returning to their homes, was for the women and
men to go separately, and the infants or children to go with
either parent indiscriminately. And so both Mary and Joseph
each thought in turn that the child Jesus, Whom they saw not
with them, was returning with the other parent. (ST. BEDE)

4. But why did they seek Him in sorrow? Was it that He might
have perished or been lost? It could not be. For what should
cause them to dread the loss of Him whom they knew to be
the Lord? No, they sought Jesus, lest perhaps, leaving them
behind, He might have returned to heaven, to descend at
another place or time. And so, the one who seeks Jesus must
go about it not carelessly and idly, as many do, and as a result
never find Him, but rather, Christ ought to be sought with
labour and sorrow lest He might pass them by. (ORIGEN)

5. Because moreover He was the Son of God, He is found
in the midst of the doctors, enlightening and instructing
them. But because He was a little child, He is found among
them not teaching but asking questions. He did this as a
duty of reverence, that He might set us an example of the
proper behaviour of children, who, even if they are wise and

learned, ought to listen to their masters' instructions rather than teach them, and ought not to vaunt themselves with empty boasting. And yet the boy Jesus asked not that He might learn, but that asking He might instruct. For from the same source of learning is derived both the ability to ask wisely and to answer wisely. (ORIGEN)

6. He is not found as soon as He was sought for, for Jesus was not among His kinsfolk and relations, among those who were joined to Him according to the flesh, nor was He in the company of the multitude. Learn where those who seek Him find Him, not everywhere, but in the temple. And so you likewise seek Jesus in the temple of God. Seek Him in the Church, and seek Him among the masters who are in the temple. They did not find Him among His kinsfolk, for human relations cannot comprehend the Son of God, nor among His acquaintances, for He passes far beyond all human knowledge and understanding. Where then do they find Him? In the temple! If at any time you seek the Son of God, seek Him first in the temple, go there, and truly shall you find Christ, the Word and the Wisdom. (ORIGEN)

7. The ever-wonderful Mother of God, moved by a mother's feelings, with weeping, makes her mournful inquiry, in every thing like a mother, with confidence, humility, and affection. As it follows, "And His mother said to Him, 'Son, what have You done to us?'" (TENTH CENTURY, 'THE GREEK EXPOSITOR')

8. The Virgin, whether she understood or whether she could not yet understand, equally laid up all things in her heart for reflection and diligent examination. Mary, the wisest of mothers, the mother of True Wisdom, becomes the student

and disciple of the Child. For she yielded to Him not as to a boy, nor as to a man, but as unto God. Further, she pondered upon His divine words and works, so that nothing that was said or done by Him was lost upon her, but as the Word Itself was previously carried in her womb, so now, in a like manner, she nurses His works and His ways in her heart, and this was her constant rule and law throughout her entire life. (ST. BEDE)

9. Let us then also ourselves be subject to our superiors. Jesus the Son of God is subject to Joseph and Mary. I must be subject to the bishop who has been constituted my father. It seems that Joseph knew that Jesus was greater than him, and for that reason in awe he moderated his authority. And so, let every one see that often the one who is subject is the greater. If those of you who are higher in dignity understand this, you will not be elated with pride, knowing that your superior may be subject to you. (ORIGEN)

10. But from His very first years being obedient to His parents, He endured all bodily labours, humbly and reverently. For since His parents were honest and just, yet at the same time poor, and ill supplied with the necessaries of life, (as His holy birth in the stable bears witness) it is plain that they continually underwent bodily fatigue in providing for their daily wants. But Jesus, being obedient to them, even to the point of carrying out laborious work, submitted Himself to them completely. (ST. BASIL THE GREAT)

GLORY BE TO THE FATHER   Glory be to the Father, and to the Son, and to the Holy Spirit, as it was in the beginning, is now and ever shall be, world without end. Amen.

THE FATIMA PRAYER   O my Jesus, forgive us our sins, save us from the fires of hell, lead all souls to heaven, especially those in most need of Thy mercy.

CONCLUDING PRAYERS   *Upon completing the recitation of the Holy Rosary, the following prayers are customary, but others too may be added according to one's devotion and preference.*

HAIL HOLY QUEEN PRAYER   Hail Holy Queen, Mother of Mercy, hail our life, our sweetness and our hope. To thee do we cry, poor banished children of Eve, to thee do we send up our sighs, mourning and weeping in this vale of tears. Turn then, most gracious advocate, thine eyes of mercy towards us, and after this, our exile, show unto us the blessed fruit of thy womb, Jesus. O clement, O loving, O sweet Virgin Mary. Pray for us O holy Mother of God, that we may be made worthy of the promises of Christ.

Let Us Pray   O God, Whose only begotten son, by His life, death and resurrection, has purchased for us the rewards of eternal life, grant we beseech Thee, that meditating on these mysteries of the most Holy Rosary of the Blessed Virgin Mary, we may both imitate what they contain and obtain what they promise, through the same Christ our Lord. Amen.

SAINT MICHAEL THE ARCHANGEL PRAYER   Holy Michael, the Archangel, defend us in the day of battle. Be our safeguard against the wickedness and snares of the devil. May God rebuke him, we humbly pray; and do thou, O Prince of the heavenly hosts, by the power of God thrust down into hell Satan and all the evil spirits who wander through the world seeking the ruin of souls. Amen.

MEMORARE PRAYER   Remember, O most gracious Virgin Mary, that never was it known that anyone who fled to thy protection, implored thy help, or sought thine intercession was left unaided. Inspired by this confidence, I fly unto thee, O Virgin of virgins, my mother; to thee do I come, before thee I stand, sinful and sorrowful. O Mother of the Word Incarnate, despise not my petitions, but in thy mercy hear and answer me. Amen.

May the Divine Assistance remain always with us, and may the souls of the faithful departed, through the mercy of God rest in peace. Amen.

The Sorrowful Mysteries

The Agony of Our Lord in the Garden

THE FRUIT OF THIS MYSTERY

The grace of perseverance in prayer during times of trial

URING THE NIGHT THE traitor appeared, bringing with him the servants of the Jews together with the band of soldiers. Judas thought that he would take the Lord even against His will, expecting a resistance from the number of Christ's followers. Christ, then, in order to show that Judas had been regarding Him as a mere man, and that his plans were vain, anticipates their attack and goes out readily to meet them, showing thereby that He well knew what Judas presumed to attempt, and that, though it were easy for Him, through His foreknowledge, to escape unawares, He went freely meet His sufferings. He asks those who have come to capture Him who they have come in search of, not because He did not know (for how could that be?), but that He might prove that those who were gazing upon Him, were not able so much as to recognise Him unless He had of His own will permitted it. The divine dignity of Christ is seen, Who brought Himself to those who were seeking Him, though they couldn't themselves recognise Him. And that He might show the fruitlessness of numbers, and the utter incapacity of all human power to affect anything against the ineffable power of God, by merely addressing them in mild and courteous language He bows down to the earth the multitude of those who sought Him. See how powerless is the nature of created beings before Almighty God, they are unable to bear but one word of His, and that spoken in kindness. (ST. CYRIL OF ALEXANDRIA)

OUR FATHER   Our Father, Who art in Heaven, hallowed be Thy name, Thy kingdom come, Thy will be done, on earth as it is in heaven. Give us this day our daily bread; and forgive us our trespasses, as we forgive those who trespass against us; and lead us not into temptation, but deliver us from evil. Amen.

HAIL MARY (10)   Hail Mary, Full of Grace, the Lord is with thee. Blessed art thou among women and blessed is the fruit of thy womb, Jesus. Holy Mary, Mother of God, pray for us sinners now, and at the hour of our death. Amen.

1. And Judas, going into the sanctuary at the dawn of the fifth day, said to Elders, "What will you give me if I am able to deliver over to you the overthrower of the law, and the plunderer of the prophets?" The Jews replied, "If you will give Him up to us, we will give you thirty pieces." And Judas received the money. Judas continued to follow Christ, not that he might be obedient to the miracles done by Him, nor that he might confess Him, but that he might betray Him to the Jews. As evening approached, Judas said to them again, "Give me the aid of soldiers with swords and staves, and I will give Him up to you." They therefore gave Judas officers for the purpose of seizing the Christ, and Judas said to them, "Lay hold of the man I kiss" (SIXTH CENTURY, THE NARRATIVE OF JOSEPH OF ARIMATHEA)

2. It was the Lord's custom always to pray by Himself, in order to give us an example, to seek for silence and solitude in our prayers. But this time it follows, "and He took with Him Peter, James and John". He takes with Him those who had been witnesses of His glory on Mount Tabor, that they who had seen His glory might also see His sufferings, and learn that He is really man. For since He had taken on Himself the whole of human nature, He took also those natural things which belong to man; heaviness, sorrow and even human nature's shrinking away from death. (THEOPHYLACT)

3. The Lord took with Him the self-confident Peter, and the others, that they might see Him falling on His face and praying, and might learn not to think great things, but little things of themselves, and not to be hasty in promising, but careful in prayer. And then, "He went forward a little," not to go far from them, but that He might still be near them

as He prayed. And even though Jesus only went but a "little forward", they could not watch one hour in His absence, let us therefore pray that Jesus may never depart even the smallest distance from us. (ORIGEN)

4. And as He began to have fear and sorrow, He prayed accordingly that the cup of His Passion might pass from Him. Likewise, the believer may in the first instance be loth to suffer pain, seeing it leads to death, and he is a man of flesh; but if it be God's will, he submits because he is a believer. For as we ought not to be too confident, lest we make a foolish boast of our own strength; so neither ought we to be distrustful, lest we should seem to charge God our helper with weakness. (ORIGEN)

5. Some say that the Angel spoke to Christ in the garden with words of praise, saying, "Yours O Lord is the power, for truly You are able to vanquish death, and to deliver weak mankind." But it was also for our benefit, to make known to us the power of prayer so that we might have recourse to it in adversity, for when our Lord prays He is comforted by an Angel. (THEOPHYLACT)

6. As soon as He said to the soldiers, "I am He", they went backwards. Where now is the band of soldiers? Where now is the terror and the threat of arms? Without a blow, struck solely by a word, they are driven back. The Lord pulls to the floor a crowd fierce with hatred, terrible with arms. What shall He do when He comes to judge, Who did thus when He was going to be judged? And now, even at the present time Christ continues to say by the Gospel, "I am He", and the unbelievers, like the Jews of old, go backwards, they fall

to the ground, because forsaking heavenly things, they cling only to things of earth. (ST. AUGUSTINE)

7. O great manifestation of Divine power, great discipline of virtue! Both the design of Your traitor is detected, and yet forbearance is not withheld. Our Lord kissed him, not in any pretence, but to show that He would not even shrink from a traitor, and that He might the more move him by not denying him the offices of love. He says, "Do you betray Me with a kiss?", that is, "Do you inflict a wound with the pledge of love? With the instruments of peace do you impose death? A slave, do you betray your Lord? A disciple, your master? One chosen, do you betray Him Who chose you?" (ST. AMBROSE)

8. Now that all obstacles had been overcome, and Peter had put away his sword, and Christ had, as it were, surrendered Himself to the hand of the Jews, (though He might have easily escaped), the soldiers and servants give way to cruel rage, and are filled with the ardour of victory. They took the Lord, Who had given Himself up wholly to their will, and put fetters upon Him, though He came to us to release us from the bondage of the devil, and to loose us from the chains of sin. (ST. CYRIL OF ALEXANDRIA)

9. Who would not marvel? Who would not give glory? When the slaves had sinned the Master was given up. The sons of perdition and the children of darkness went out in the darkness to arrest The Sun, Who had the power to consume them in an instant. But the Master, knowing their effrontery and the force of their anger, with gentleness, by His own authority, gave Himself up into the hands of the ungodly. And lawless men, having bound the most pure Master, mocked the One

Who had bound the strong one with unbreakable bonds, and set us free from the bonds of sins. (ST. EPHREM)

10. And it was thus that Divine Providence permitted Peter to fall first, in order that he might be less severe to sinners from the remembrance of his own fall. Peter, the teacher and master of the whole world, sinned, and obtained pardon. For this reason I suppose the priesthood was not given to angels, because, being without sin themselves, they would punish sinners without pity. Instead, passible, sinful, men are placed over other men, in order that remembering their own weakness, they might be merciful to others. (ST. JOHN CHRYSOSTOM)

GLORY BE TO THE FATHER   Glory be to the Father, and to the Son, and to the Holy Spirit, as it was in the beginning, is now and ever shall be, world without end. Amen.

THE FATIMA PRAYER   O my Jesus, forgive us our sins, save us from the fires of hell, lead all souls to heaven, especially those in most need of Thy mercy.

The Scourging of Our Lord at the Pillar

THE FRUIT OF THIS MYSTERY

A more determined mortification of the flesh

EE THE LORD IS made ready for the scourge, see now it descends upon Him! That sacred skin is torn by the fury of the rods, the cruel might of repeated blows lacerates His shoulders. God is stretched out before man, and He, in Whom not one trace of sin can be discerned, suffers punishment as an evil doer. (ST. JOHN CHRYSOSTOM)

OUR FATHER   Our Father, Who art in Heaven, hallowed be Thy name, Thy kingdom come, Thy will be done, on earth as it is in heaven. Give us this day our daily bread; and forgive us our trespasses, as we forgive those who trespass against us; and lead us not into temptation, but deliver us from evil. Amen.

HAIL MARY (10)   Hail Mary, Full of Grace, the Lord is with thee. Blessed art thou among women and blessed is the fruit of thy womb, Jesus. Holy Mary, Mother of God, pray for us sinners now, and at the hour of our death. Amen.

1. The Virgin uttered affectionate wailing in the house of John when they brought to her the sad news of her son's mistreatment. And so she began to look for one of His holy disciples to walk with her to see Him, but she could not find any, because all had fled and forsaken Him from fear of the Jews. She asked for Peter to accompany her, and she was informed that from his fear of the High Priest he had denied her Son, saying, "I do not know Him," and that he had gone and hidden himself from Him. She asked for James, who was their kindred, and she was informed that he had fled and left Him on the mount where He was seized. She asked for Thomas, and she was informed that he had thrown down his garments and fled. Indeed, She asked for each of them by name, and not a single one of them was willing to go, only John, the beloved, and so he accompanied her. (FIFTH CENTURY, PSEUDO GAMALIEL)

2. And having laid hold of the Lord and bound Him, they led Him to the house of Caiaphas the high priest wherein was assembled a great rout, not a holy council, but an assembly of the wicked and a council of the ungodly. And when the soldiers gave Him up to Caiaphas and the chief priests, Judas said, "This is Him, the One Who stole the law and the prophets." And the Jews gave Jesus an unjust trial, saying, "Why have You done these things?" And He gave no answer. These Jews did many evil things against Him, and left no kind of injury untried, spitting upon Him, beating Him, striking Him on the face, reviling Him, tempting Him, seeking vain divination instead of true prophecies from Him. They called Him a deceiver, a blasphemer, a transgressor of Moses, a destroyer of the temple, a taker away of sacrifices, an enemy to the Romans, and adversary to Caesar. These bulls and dogs in their madness cast such reproaches upon Him unceasingly, till it was very early in the morning. (SIXTH CENTURY, THE NARRATIVE OF JOSEPH OF ARIMATHEA)

3. Behold how the devil held them all in his grasp, convincing them to commit murder on such high days when they ought to have been making many sacrifices and offerings for their other sins, and for their purification and cleansing. But instead they bound Him and led Him away to Pilate the governor. The mendacious chief priests and the elders handed the Lord over to Pilate on the grounds that He was leading a rebellion and had been plotting against the emperor. (THEOPHYLACT)

4. "And He stood before the unworthy high priest, and from there He was handed over to Pilate. And they laid every kind of torment on Him, but He, as a lamb stands silent before

the shearer, so He does not open His mouth." * (ST. MAXIMUS THE CONFESSOR)

5. O, how miraculous! While being judged by Pilate, Christ caused his wife to suffer a fright. It was not Pilate who saw the dream, but his wife, either because he was unworthy, or because the people would not have believed that he had seen such a dream and would think that he said this only with a view to granting a pardon. Or perhaps he would have kept silent if he had seen it. The dream was, still, a work of providence, not occurring so that Christ would be released, but so that a woman might be saved. Pilate, however, allowed himself to be drawn to the side of the Jews, like one who is mute and cowardly, and because of this he is not without blame. Pilate washed his hands as if to show that he was clean of defilement, but his thoughts were evil. For he called Jesus a righteous man and yet handed Him over be scourged, that is, he had Him whipped, either to gratify the people, or else to show that it was he himself who had condemned Christ, and to make it appear that they were not about to crucify an innocent man, but rather one who was dishonourable. (THEOPHYLACT)

6. It was as if the Lord said, "Whoever you are, approaching and entering the precincts of the middle of the temple, stop a little and look upon Me, Who, though innocent, suffered for your crime, lay Me up in your mind, keep Me in your breast. I am He Who, pitying the bitter misfortunes of men,

---

* Maximus the Confessor, *"The Life of the Virgin"*, (Yale: Bloomsbury 2012), 103.

came here as a messenger offering peace and a full atonement for the sins of men." Behold, here is the merciful image of salvation. (LACTANTIUS)

7. Come, observe well the abundance of compassion, the forbearance and mercy of our sweet Master. He had a useful slave in the paradise of delight, and when the slave sinned he was given over to the torturers. But when the Good One saw the slave's weakness of soul He took compassion on the him, and had mercy on him and presented Himself to be scourged. (ST. EPHREM)

8. Note well, that when Jesus is scourged and spat upon, He does not wear His own garments, but rather, those which He took upon Himself for our sins. (ST. JEROME)

9. The Cherubim at the throne hid their faces behind it and the Seraphim struck their wings all at once, at that moment, when the creature gave a blow to its Master. How did earth's foundations endure the earthquake and the tremor at that moment, when the Master was outraged? I observe, and I tremble, and again I am stunned, when I see the long-suffering of the loving Master. Indeed, my very insides quiver as I speak, because the Creator, Who by grace fashioned humanity from dust, He the Fashioner is struck. Let us fear, my brethren and not simply listen. The Saviour endured all these things for us. (ST. EPHREM)

10. But the people, like wild beasts that rage the open plains, wanted Barabbas released to them. Seditions, murders and robberies are practised and nourished by all who do not believe devoutly in the Lord Jesus. Where Jesus is not, there is strife

and violence. Where He is, there is peace and all good things. All those who are like these Jews in either doctrine or life desire Barabbas to be loosed to them, for whosoever does evil loosens Barabbas in himself, and Jesus is bound; but he that does good has Christ loosed, and Barabbas bound. (ORIGEN)

GLORY BE TO THE FATHER   Glory be to the Father, and to the Son, and to the Holy Spirit, as it was in the beginning, is now and ever shall be, world without end. Amen.

THE FATIMA PRAYER   O my Jesus, forgive us our sins, save us from the fires of hell, lead all souls to heaven, especially those in most need of Thy mercy.

The Crowning with Thorns

THE FRUIT OF THIS MYSTERY

Detachment from the charms of this world and from all worldly esteem

HEY SCOURGE HIM UNJUSTLY, and the Lord suffers the crowd of soldiers to insult Him, to put a crown of thorns about His head, to throw a purple robe upon Him, to beat Him with the palms of their hands and to otherwise dishonour Him. Pilate thought he could easily put to shame the Jews if they saw the Man Who was altogether free from guilt suffering such a punishment without a cause. Jesus was scourged unjustly, that He might deliver us from merited chastisement. He was bruised and beaten, that we might fight Satan, who attacks us, and that we might escape from the sin that cleaves to us through the original transgression. For if we think correctly, we shall realise that all Christ's sufferings were for us and on our behalf, and that they have the power to release and deliver us from all those calamities that we have deserved in rebelling against God. (ST. CYRIL OF ALEXANDRIA)

OUR FATHER   Our Father, Who art in Heaven, hallowed be Thy name, Thy kingdom come, Thy will be done, on earth as it is in heaven. Give us this day our daily bread; and forgive us our trespasses, as we forgive those who trespass against us; and lead us not into temptation, but deliver us from evil. Amen.

HAIL MARY (10)   Hail Mary, Full of Grace, the Lord is with thee. Blessed art thou among women and blessed is the fruit of thy womb, Jesus. Holy Mary, Mother of God, pray for us sinners now, and at the hour of our death. Amen.

1. Pilate ordered his officers to bring him water. Washing his hands, he said to the people, "I am innocent of the blood of this good man. See to it yourselves that He is unjustly put to death, since I have not found a fault in Him, nor has Herod; for because of this he has sent Him back again to me." The Jews said, "His blood be upon us, and upon our children." Then Pilate sat down upon his throne to pass sentence. He gave orders, and Jesus came before him. And they brought a crown of thorns, and put it on His head, and a reed into His right hand. Then he passed sentence, and said to Him, "Your nation testifies against You that You desire to be a king.

Therefore I judge that first, You should be beaten for forty strokes with a rod, as the law of the kings' decrees, and then that You shall be mocked, and that finally, You shall be crucified" (THIRD CENTURY, THE ACTS OF PILATE)

2. They plaited a crown of their own thorns, the fruit borne by the vine of the Jews. In mockery they called Him 'King'. The lawless spat in the face of the most pure, at Whose glance all the powers of heaven and the ranks of angels quake with fear. (ST. EPHREM)

3. For instead of a diadem, they put upon Him a crown of thorns, and a purple robe to represent the purple robe which kings wear. And though the soldiers did this in mockery, yet to us their acts have a meaning. For by the crown of thorns is signified the taking of our sins upon Him, the thorns which the earth of our body brings forth. And the purple robe signifies the flesh crucified. (ST. BEDE)

4. What should we care from now on if anyone insults us, after Christ has suffered like this? The utmost that cruel outrage could do was put in practice against Christ, and not only on one of His members, but His whole body suffered injuries; His head from the crown, the reed, and the buffetings; His face which was spat upon; His cheeks which they struck with the palms of their hands; His whole body from the scourging, the stripping and the mockery of homage; His hands from the reed which they put into them as a mimicry of a sceptre. It was as though they were afraid of leaving any part of Him without indignity. (ST. JOHN CHRYSOSTOM)

5. They hit the head of Christ with a reed who speak against His divinity, and endeavour to maintain their error by the authority of Holy Scripture, which is written by a reed. They spit upon His face who reject in abominable words the presence of His grace and deny that Jesus has come in the flesh. And they mock Him with adoration who pledge to believe in Him, but despise Him with perverse works. (RABANUS MAURUS)

6. The soldiers clothed Him with a cloak as if it were the imperial purple, they gave Him a reed for a sceptre and a crown of thorns for a diadem, they paid Him homage in mockery. But if they did these things in derision, you must understand them also in a more spiritual manner, as something not merely done to, but also accomplished by Jesus. The scarlet cloak reveals our nature, bloody and murderous, which He assumed and sanctified by wearing it. The crown is made of thorns which are the sins resulting from our cares for this life, these Christ consumes with His own divinity, for His head represents His divinity. The reed is a symbol of our weak and crumbling nature which the Lord assumed. By receiving insults in His ears, He healed Eve of the whispering of the serpent which had entered her ears. (THEOPHYLACT)

7. Jesus goes forth to the people not resplendent in kingly power but laden with reproach, with the words, "Behold the man!" It was as if Pilate was saying to them, "If you hate your king, spare Him now that you see Him sunk so low; He has been scourged, crowned with thorns, clothed with the garments of derision, jeered at with the bitterest insults, struck with the open hand; His dishonour is at the boiling point, let your ill-will sink to zero." But there is no such

cooling on their part, but rather a further increase of heat and vehemence. (ST. AUGUSTINE)

8. The crowd of the common people were brought somewhat to shame by the sight of Christ's sufferings, as they called to mind the wonderful miracles that He had performed. Then, however, their rulers began to clamour, and in doing so to kindle into a strange fury the passions of these common people. That which was said in the prophets, concerning them, is true, "For the pastors have become brutish, and have not sought the Lord; therefore all their flock perceived Him not, and are scattered abroad." The origin of this most evil crime was with the Jewish leaders who purposed to put the Lord of the Vineyard to death, hoping to securely enjoy His heritage, thinking that if Christ were removed, that they would once again rule and enjoy all honour. (ST. CYRIL OF ALEXANDRIA)

9. My heart trembles as I think on these things: the slave is seated, the Master stands, and one full of iniquities passes sentence on the One Who is sinless. (ST. EPHREM)

10. "With the eyes and ears of the flesh the Virgin Mary saw and heard the judgments that were put forth against Him, but mentally she was joined to her sweet Son and what was happening to Him. She was pierced in her heart because everyone had turned away all at once through weakness and cowardice. Those who were committing the transgression did

not understand, and they condemned the Life of All Things to death." * (ST. MAXIMUS THE CONFESSOR)

GLORY BE TO THE FATHER   Glory be to the Father, and to the Son, and to the Holy Spirit, as it was in the beginning, is now and ever shall be, world without end. Amen.

THE FATIMA PRAYER   O my Jesus, forgive us our sins, save us from the fires of hell, lead all souls to heaven, especially those in most need of Thy mercy.

---

*   Maximus the Confessor, *The Life of the Virgin*, (Yale: Bloomsbury 2012), 104

The Carrying of the Cross

THE FRUIT OF THIS MYSTERY

A greater love of the cross, to embrace the necessary means of salvation

THEY COMPEL JESUS TO bear the cross, regarding it as unholy, and therefore avoiding the touch of it themselves. And He, bearing His cross, went forth to a place called the place of a skull, which is called in Hebrew Golgotha, where they crucified Him. The same was prefigured by Isaac, who carried the wood. But Isaac only continued as his father's good pleasure ordered, but now the deed was fully accomplished, for the reality had appeared. (ST. JOHN CHRYSOSTOM)

OUR FATHER   Our Father, Who art in Heaven, hallowed be Thy name, Thy kingdom come, Thy will be done, on earth as it is in heaven. Give us this day our daily bread; and forgive us our trespasses, as we forgive those who trespass against us; and lead us not into temptation, but deliver us from evil. Amen.

HAIL MARY (10)   Hail Mary, Full of Grace, the Lord is with thee. Blessed art thou among women and blessed is the fruit of thy womb, Jesus. Holy Mary, Mother of God, pray for us sinners now, and at the hour of our death. Amen.

1. Pilate saw then that it was all in vain and said to them, "Take Him yourselves and crucify Him." This is the speech of a man abhorring the deed and urging others to do a deed which he abhors himself. They had brought Our Lord to him that He might be put to death by his sentence, but the result was the opposite, the governor acquitted Him saying, "I find no fault in Him." Pilate clears Him immediately from all charges, which shows that he had only permitted the former outrages to humour the madness of the Jews. But nothing could shame the Jewish hounds, and so they answered him, "We have a law, and by our law He ought to die, because He made Himself the Son of God." (ST. JOHN CHRYSOSTOM)

2. Jesus, therefore, went to the place where He was to be crucified, bearing His cross. A grand spectacle! For the wicked onlooker, a laughing-stock, for the pious, a deep mystery, for the wicked onlooker, a demonstration of ignominy, for the pious, a bulwark of faith. As the wicked man looks on, he

laughs at the King bearing, in place of His kingly rod, the tree of His punishment, but the pious man sees the cross, that which one day will be affixed even on the foreheads of kings, and which the hearts of the saints will desire after. (ST. AUGUSTINE)

3. And so the Lord was handed over to their savage wishes, and in mockery of His kingly state, ordered to be the bearer of His own instrument of death, that what Isaiah the prophet foresaw might be fulfilled, saying, "Behold a Child is born for us, a Son is given to us and the government is laid upon His shoulders." When, therefore, the Lord carried the wood of the cross, which should turn for Him into the sceptre of power, it was indeed in the eyes of the wicked a mighty mockery, but to the faithful a mighty mystery was set forth. He, the glorious vanquisher of the Devil, and the strong defeater of the powers that were against Him, was nobly carrying the trophy of His triumph, and on the shoulders of His unconquered patience bore for all to see the adorable sign of salvation. In doing so He charged His followers saying, "He that does not take up his cross and follow Me is not worthy of Me." (ST. LEO THE GREAT)

4. And Mary said, "I beg you, O John, to show me the way to the Calvary. I adjure you, O John, to accompany me to the Golgotha. I have never yet seen a robber being crucified, nor have I stood near a robber when he was being beheaded. I shall go bare-footed to the place in which my beloved Son is being crucified like a common robber, because He is alone and none of His brethren are standing near Him. My sorrow, O my child, is today greater than that of all the world, and of all the inhabitants of Jerusalem, and my weeping is more

bitter than that of all who shall gather near me." (FIFTH
CENTURY, PSEUDO GAMALIEL)

5. The Virgin, therefore, walked through the streets of Jerusalem towards the place of execution. The people who saw the
Virgin passing by said to one another, "From where is this
wailing woman?" And the market traders said, "We have never
seen this woman buying anything from our stores." Others
said, "This is a foreign woman, for she walks in this streets
as if she doesn't know them." Some men who recognised in
John the disciple of the Lord Jesus, said, "This may perhaps
be the mother going to see Her Son being Crucified." Some
were saying, "Look at her, how beautiful her is face even
amidst her tears," and others, "her face resembles that of her
Son." (FIFTH CENTURY, PSEUDO GAMALIEL)

6. Open your heart, learn in detail His sufferings and say to
yourself, God Who is without sin today was given up, today
was mocked, today was abused, today was struck, today was
scourged, today wore a crown of thorns, today was taken to
be crucified, He, the heavenly Lamb. Your heart will tremble,
your soul will shudder. Shed tears every day by this meditation on the Master's sufferings. Tears become sweet, the soul
is enlightened that always meditates on Christ's sufferings.
Always meditate in this way, shedding tears every day, giving thanks to the Master for the sufferings that He suffered
for you, so that on the day of His Coming your tears may
become your boast and exaltation before the judgement seat.
(ST. EPHREM)

7. The Cross makes a man young again after he has grown old.
The Cross purifies the man that pursues the energies issuing

forth from it. The Cross is the holy mystery at the holy table bringing not bread or wine but holy body and blood. The Cross is the consolation of those who are in distress because of their sins. The Cross is the straight way, not leading astray those who walk by it. The Cross is the high tower which receives those who are running to it. The Cross is the ladder which raises man to the sky. The Cross is the garment which the Christians are wearing. The Cross is the helper of the poor and those who are distressed. The Cross is the judge of the widows, wiping out the tears from their eyes. The Cross is the physician who cures every sickness. The Cross is the chastity of the virgins. The Cross is the fortified wall. The Cross is the companion of those who are in the desert. The Cross is the consolation of pilgrims. The Cross destroys demons and casts them away in fear. (ST. THEOPHILUS OF ALEXANDRIA)

8. The one who knows God will follow the Lord's footsteps, bearing the cross of the Saviour. The Lord says, "He who loses his life will save it." We can "lose our lives" in one of two ways. First, we can risk our lives just as the Lord did for us, by dying as martyrs. Secondly, we can "lose our lives" by separating our lives from the customary things of this world. Bearing the cross means to separate your soul from the delights and pleasures of this life. If you do this, you will find your life again, resting in the hope of what is to come. Dying to yourself means being content with the necessities of life, for wanting more than these necessities is the easy route to sin. (ST. CLEMENT OF ALEXANDRIA)

9. To begin with Jesus carried the cross alone as no one else was willing to carry it, but along the way they found Simon and placed the cross on him. You, O reader, learn this as well,

that "Simon" means "obedience", therefore he who possesses obedience is he who carries the cross of Christ. And Cyrene was one of the five cities of the Pentapolis, signifying the five senses that are compelled to bear the cross. (THEOPHYLACT)

10. Now it is the time for the Victorious One to erect His trophy. The Cross is placed on His shoulders like a trophy. Whether it be Simon or the Lord who wears it, Christ carried it into man, and man carried it into Christ. Again, see how it reflects the progress of history, the Lord first held up Himself the trophy of His Cross, then He gave it to the martyrs to lift. It is not a Jew who carries the Cross, but a stranger of passage. He does not precede, but follows, as it is written, "Take up your cross and follow Me." (ST. AMBROSE)

GLORY BE TO THE FATHER   Glory be to the Father, and to the Son, and to the Holy Spirit, as it was in the beginning, is now and ever shall be, world without end. Amen.

THE FATIMA PRAYER   O my Jesus, forgive us our sins, save us from the fires of hell, lead all souls to heaven, especially those in most need of Thy mercy.

The Death of Our Lord on the Cross

THE FRUIT OF THIS MYSTERY

The grace of a happy death, fortified by the sacraments of the church

I T WAS AS IF Jesus said, "See the immense cross pressing My shoulders and wearied back, watch My painful steps to a dreadful death. Survey Me from head to foot, deserted as I am, lifted up afar from My beloved mother. Behold and see My hair clotted with blood, My blood-stained neck, My head drained of its blood by cruel thorns and a stream of blood pouring down like rain over My divine face. Survey My compressed and sightless eyes, My afflicted cheeks, see My parched tongue poisoned with gall and My countenance pale with death. Behold My hands pierced with nails, My arms drawn out, My perforated feet, the great wound in My side; see the blood streaming from it and My blood-stained limbs. Bend your knee, and with lamentation adore the venerable wood of the cross, with a lowly countenance sprinkle the earth with your tears. Continually guard Me and My teachings in your devoted heart." (LACTANTIUS)

OUR FATHER   Our Father, Who art in Heaven, hallowed be Thy name, Thy kingdom come, Thy will be done, on earth as it is in heaven. Give us this day our daily bread; and forgive us our trespasses, as we forgive those who trespass against us; and lead us not into temptation, but deliver us from evil. Amen.

HAIL MARY (10)   Hail Mary, Full of Grace, the Lord is with thee. Blessed art thou among women and blessed is the fruit of thy womb, Jesus. Holy Mary, Mother of God, pray for us sinners now, and at the hour of our death. Amen.

1. The passers by blasphemed Christ, reproaching Him as a fraud. But the devil moved them to bid Him to come down from the Cross, for he knew that salvation was being won by the Cross, and therefore he again proceeded to tempt Christ, so that if He came down from the Cross, he might be certain that He was not truly the Son of God, and so the salvation, which is by the Cross, might be done away with. But the Lord Jesus, being truly the Son of God, did not come down. He saw that it was through this way that salvation must be

effected, and so He underwent the crucifixion and many other sufferings in order to accomplish His work. (THEOPHYLACT)

2. Indeed, even the cross, if you consider it, was a judgment seat, for the Judge was in the middle, one thief, who believed, was pardoned, the other, who mocked, was damned. Here is a sign of what He will one day do to the living and the dead, placing the one on His right hand, the other on His left. (ST. AUGUSTINE)

3. What power, O thief, led you to the light? Who taught you to worship that despised man, your companion on the Cross? O Light Eternal, Which gives light to those who are in darkness! O mighty and ineffable grace! The faithful Abraham had not yet entered, but the thief enters. Moses and the Prophets had not yet entered, and the thief enters even though once a breaker of the law. St. Paul wondered at this, saying, "Where sin abounded, there grace abounded even more." They who had borne the heat of the day had not yet entered, but he of the eleventh hour enters. (ST. CYRIL OF JERUSALEM)

4. The garment which cannot be torn, the garment without seam, denotes the body of Christ, which was woven from above by the power of the Holy Ghost over the Virgin. This holy body of Christ then is indivisible, and though it may be distributed for every one to partake of, and to sanctify the soul and body of each one individually, yet it subsists in each person fully and indivisibly. (THEOPHYLACT)

5. As to the Virgin, she inclined her face towards the earth on account of her weeping and humility, and she was not able to see her Son easily because of her painful weeping and the

thronging of the great multitudes of people. And so she said to John, "Where is my beloved Son so that I may see Him? The pressing of this crowd of people against one another does not allow me to see Him." And John said to her, "Lift your head towards the western side of these people, and you will see Him extended on the cross." And the Virgin looked though the whole crowd of people, and she saw Him. She did not cease to wade with John through the multitudes until she came and stood at His right, and looked at Him in His sufferings. (FIFTH CENTURY, PSEUDO GAMALIEL)

6. When God saw His mother He looked towards John and said to him, "O man, this is your mother", and then He said to His mother, "O mother, this is your son." And John held the Virgin's hand in order to take her to his house, but the Virgin, his mother, said, "O John, let me weep over Him as He has no brother and no sister, do not deprive me of Him. O my Son, would that I had with You a crown of thorns on my head, and would that I could make it as painful as Yours. O John, look at my wretchedness today in the middle of these multitudes. Look at my lowliness and at the pains of my heart." (FIFTH CENTURY, PSEUDO GAMALIEL)

7. Mary, the mother of our Lord, stood before the cross of her Son. None of the Evangelists has told me this except John. The others have related how at our Lord's Passion the earth quaked, the heaven was overspread with darkness, the sun fled and that the thief was taken into paradise after confession. John has told us, what the others have not, how that from the cross upon which He hung, He called to His mother. John thought it a greater thing to recall Christ fulfilling the offices of piety to His mother, than giving the kingdom of heaven

and eternal life to the thief. For if it was a religious work to give life to the thief, it was a much richer work of piety for the Son to honour His mother with such affection. "Behold your son" He says, "Behold your mother." Christ made His last testament from the cross, and divided the offices of piety between the Mother and the disciple. Mary, as became the Mother of our Lord, stood before the cross after the Apostles had fled, and with pitiful eyes beheld the wounds of her Son. But she looked not on the death of a hostage, but on the salvation of the world. (ST. AMBROSE)

8. Wonder! What honour He pays to the disciple He loved, the evangelist, who conceals his name from modesty. What honour in giving him such a charge, to have the mother of our Lord, in her affliction, committed to his care at the moment of the Lord's departure, for thus He says to the disciple, "Behold your mother!" (ST. JOHN CHRYSOSTOM)

9. Pay attention, all families of the nations, and observe! An extraordinary murder has taken place in the centre of Jerusalem, in the city devoted to God's law, in the city of the Hebrews, in the city of the prophets, in the city thought of as just. And Who has been murdered? And who is the murderer? I am ashamed to give the answer, but give it I must. The One Who hung the earth in space is Himself hanged; the One Who fixed the heavens in place is Himself impaled, the One Who firmly fixed all things is Himself firmly fixed to the tree. The Lord is insulted, God has been murdered, the King of Israel has been destroyed by the right hand of Israel. O frightful murder! O unheard of injustice! The Lord is disfigured and He is not deemed worthy of a cloak for His naked body. For this reason the stars turned and fled and the day grew quite

dark, in order to hide the naked figure hanging on the tree, darkening not the body of the Lord, but the eyes of men. Yes, even though the people did not tremble, the earth trembled instead. Although the people were not afraid, the heavens grew frightened. Although the people did not tear their garments, the angels tore theirs. Although the people did not lament, the Lord thundered from heaven and the Most High uttered His voice. (ST. MELITO OF SARDIS)

10. Shameless man, do you watch the most pure Master hanging on the Cross, while you pass the time that you have to live on earth in pleasure and laughter? Don't you know, miserable wretch, that the crucified Lord will demand an account of all your disdainful deeds, for which, when you hear of them, you show no concern, and as you take your pleasure you laugh and enjoy yourself with indifference. The day will come, that fearful day, for you to weep unceasingly and to cry out in the fire from your pains. Then there will be no one at all to answer and to have mercy on your soul. But, as for me, my Lord, O Holy One, I worship You, I entreat You, I fall down before You, given over to death for me, an unworthy sinner. And now, what shall I give You in return? (ST. EPHREM)

GLORY BE TO THE FATHER   Glory be to the Father, and to the Son, and to the Holy Spirit, as it was in the beginning, is now and ever shall be, world without end. Amen.

THE FATIMA PRAYER   O my Jesus, forgive us our sins, save us from the fires of hell, lead all souls to heaven, especially those in most need of Thy mercy.

CONCLUDING PRAYERS *Upon completing the recitation of the Holy Rosary, the following prayers are customary, but others too may be added according to one's devotion and preference.*

HAIL HOLY QUEEN PRAYER Hail Holy Queen, Mother of Mercy, hail our life, our sweetness and our hope. To thee do we cry, poor banished children of Eve, to thee do we send up our sighs, mourning and weeping in this vale of tears. Turn then, most gracious advocate, thine eyes of mercy towards us, and after this, our exile, show unto us the blessed fruit of thy womb, Jesus. O clement, O loving, O sweet Virgin Mary. Pray for us O holy Mother of God, that we may be made worthy of the promises of Christ.

Let Us Pray O God, Whose only begotten son, by His life, death and resurrection, has purchased for us the rewards of eternal life, grant we beseech Thee, that meditating on these mysteries of the most Holy Rosary of the Blessed Virgin Mary, we may both imitate what they contain and obtain what they promise, through the same Christ our Lord. Amen.

SAINT MICHAEL THE ARCHANGEL PRAYER Holy Michael, the Archangel, defend us in the day of battle. Be our safeguard against the wickedness and snares of the devil. May God rebuke him, we humbly pray; and do thou, O Prince of the heavenly hosts, by the power of God thrust down into hell Satan and all the evil spirits who wander through the world seeking the ruin of souls. Amen.

MEMORARE PRAYER Remember, O most gracious Virgin Mary, that never was it known that anyone who fled to thy protection, implored thy help, or sought thine intercession was left unaided. Inspired by this confidence, I fly unto thee, O Virgin of virgins, my mother; to thee do I come, before thee I stand, sinful and sorrowful. O Mother of the Word Incarnate, despise not my petitions, but in thy mercy hear and answer me. Amen.

May the Divine Assistance remain always with us, and may the souls of the faithful departed, through the mercy of God rest in peace. Amen.

The Glorious Mysteries

The Resurrection of Our Lord from the Dead

THE FRUIT OF THIS MYSTERY

An increase of faith in the mystery of the Our Divine Lord's holy resurrection

THE WOMEN CAME TO the sepulchre and when they could not find the body of Christ, for He had risen, they were very confused. And what followed? Because of their love for Christ, and their earnest zeal towards Him, they were counted worthy of seeing holy angels. The women, having been taught the mystery by the voice of angels, run to tell these things to the disciples. It was fitting that this splendid grace should be granted to women. For she who of old was the minister of death is now freed from her guilt by ministering to the voice of the holy angels, and by being the first both to learn and tell the adorable mystery of the resurrection. Through this, women gained both acquittal from their reproach and the reversal of their curse. For the One Who in Eden had said to them, "In pains shall you bear children", now delivers them from this misfortune by meeting them in the garden. (ST. JOHN CHRYSOSTOM)

OUR FATHER   Our Father, Who art in Heaven, hallowed be Thy name, Thy kingdom come, Thy will be done, on earth as it is in heaven. Give us this day our daily bread; and forgive us our trespasses, as we forgive those who trespass against us; and lead us not into temptation, but deliver us from evil. Amen.

HAIL MARY (10)   Hail Mary, Full of Grace, the Lord is with thee. Blessed art thou among women and blessed is the fruit of thy womb, Jesus. Holy Mary, Mother of God, pray for us sinners now, and at the hour of our death. Amen.

1. Now, when all those who had fallen asleep since the beginning of the world were lying in Hades, in the blackness of darkness and shadow of death, suddenly there appeared at the hour of midnight, a golden light as of the sun, and a purple, royal light shone upon them. And as this light shone into these dark regions, those who dwelt there were all lighted up and saw each other; and Hades and the gates of death trembled. And then was heard the voice of the Son of the Father Most High, as if the voice of a great thunder; and

loudly proclaiming He thus charged them, "Lift up your gates, you princes; lift up the everlasting gates; the King of glory, Christ the Lord, is coming to enter in." (FOURTH CENTURY, PSEUDO NICODEMUS)

2. And the Lord set His cross in the midst of Hades, which is the sign of victory, and which will remain even to eternity. And the Lord, stretching forth His hand, made the sign of the cross upon Adam, upon his forehead, and upon all His saints, the patriarchs, prophets, martyrs, and forefathers; and holding Adam by the right hand, He went up from the powers below and all the saints followed Him. And as He was going, holy David cried out aloud, saying, "Sing unto the Lord a new song, for He has done wonderful things. His right hand and His holy arm have brought salvation." In like manner also, all the saints of God, falling on their knees at the feet of the Lord, said with one voice, "You have come, O Redeemer of the world. As You foretold by Your law and Your prophets, You have fulfilled their words by Your deeds. You have redeemed the living by Your cross, and by Your the death upon the cross You have come down to us, in Your majesty, to rescue us from the powers below and from unending death." (FOURTH CENTURY, PSEUDO NICODEMUS)

3. Mary Magdalene, who had been the sinner in the city, and who had washed out the spots of her sins by her tears, whose soul burned with love, did not retire from the sepulchre when the other women did. She sought the body, and did not find it. She persevered in seeking, and so it came to pass that she found. Her longings growing the stronger, the more they were disappointed, at last they found and laid hold on their object. For holy longings ever gain strength by delay. Mary so loved,

that not content with seeing the sepulchre, she stooped down and looked in. (ST. GREGORY THE GREAT)

4. The women came early in the morning to the sepulchre, from this we have an example given to us, that having cast away the darkness of our vices, we should come to the Body of the Lord. For that sepulchre also bore the figure of the altar of the Lord, where is contained mystery of Christ's Body, not in silk or purple cloth, but in pure white linen. The spices which the women bring signify the odour of virtue and the sweetness of prayers by which we ought to approach the Altar. Angels are said to have stood by, so also at the time of consecration they are believed to stand by the mysteries of Christ. Let us then, whenever we approach the heavenly mysteries, after the example of the devout women, because of the presence of the Angels, or from reverence to the Sacred Offering, with all humility, bow our faces to the earth, recollecting that we are but dust and ashes. (ST. BEDE)

5. "The other women saw the stone rolled away and the angel sitting on it; but when and how this took place, they did not know this at all. Only the immaculate Mother of the Lord standing there knew everything. And because of this, she received the good news of the Resurrection before everyone else, and before everyone else she became worthy of the longed for height of every good thing and divinely beautiful vision of her Lord and son." * (ST. MAXIMUS THE CONFESSOR)

---

* Maximus the Confessor, *"The Life of the Virgin"*, (Yale: Bloomsbury 2012), 119.

6. The disciples, when they heard what Magdalene told them, either did not believe her, or, if they believed, they grieved that the Lord did not count them worthy to have the sight of Him. But Christ did not let them pass a whole day in such reflections, and in the midst of their longing and their trembling desires to see Him, presented Himself to them. He showed Himself openly to them, and strengthened their wavering minds by His words, "peace be to you", that is, "do not be afraid", and in doing this He reminded them of what He had said before His crucifixion, "I shall see you again, and your hearts will rejoice." (ST. JOHN CHRYSOSTOM)

7. He might have, had He pleased, wiped every trace of His wounds from His glorified body, but He had reasons for retaining them. He showed them to Thomas, who would not believe except he saw and touched, and He will show them to His enemies, not to say, as He did to Thomas, "Because you have seen, you have believed", but to convict them, "Behold the Man Whom you crucified, see the wounds which you inflicted, recognise the side which you pierced, that it was by you, and for you, that it was opened, and yet you cannot enter there." Thomas saw and touched the man, and confessed the God Whom he neither saw nor touched. By means of the one he believed the other wholeheartedly, saying, "My Lord and my God." (ST. AUGUSTINE)

8. On the road to Emmaus It was necessary to test the disciples to see if, not yet loving Him as God, they were at least capable of loving Him as a traveller. Truth journeying with them, they could not remain strangers to love: they offered Him hospitality, as one does for a traveller. Moreover, they did not merely propose for Him to stay with them, but rather,

"they pressed Him". The disciples set the table, they offer food, and God, Whom they did not recognise in the explanation of Holy Scripture, they recognise in the breaking of bread. It is not by hearing the commandments of God that they have been enlightened, but by putting them into practice. Thus, whoever wants to understand what he has heard must hasten to accomplish with his works the part he has already managed to understand. As you can see, the Lord was not recognised when He spoke, but He deigned to be recognised when He was given food. Love, dear brothers, hospitality, love works inspired by charity. How lukewarm we are to practice hospitality! Consider, my brethren, what great virtue is hospitality. Receive Christ at your tables, to deserve to be received by Him at the eternal banquet. (ST. GREGORY THE GREAT)

9. When the morning came, Jesus was on the shore, but the disciples did not know it was Jesus. It may be asked, why after His resurrection He stood on the shore to receive the disciples, whereas before He walked on the sea? The sea signifies the world, which is tossed about by the waves of this corruptible life, the shore, by its solidity, signifies the rest eternal. The disciples then, inasmuch as they were still upon the waves of this mortal life, were labouring on the sea, but the Redeemer, having by His resurrection thrown off the corruption of the flesh, stood upon the shore. It is as if He wanted to use these things to speak to His disciples about the very mystery of His Resurrection, saying to them, "I do not appear to you any more on the sea, for I am no longer with you in the same sense as before." (ST. JOHN CHRYSOSTOM)

10. That which most of all attracts the divine love is care and love for our neighbour. Our Lord passing by the rest,

addresses this command to Peter, he being the chief of the Apostles, the mouth of the disciples, and head of the college. Our Lord remembers no more his sin in denying Him, or brings that as a charge against him, but commits to him at once the superintendence over his brethren. "If you love Me, have rule over your brethren, show forth that love which you have always held for them, and that life which you said you would lay down for Me, lay down for the sheep." (ST. JOHN CHRYSOSTOM)

GLORY BE TO THE FATHER   Glory be to the Father, and to the Son, and to the Holy Spirit, as it was in the beginning, is now and ever shall be, world without end. Amen.

THE FATIMA PRAYER   O my Jesus, forgive us our sins, save us from the fires of hell, lead all souls to heaven, especially those in most need of Thy mercy.

The Ascension of Our Lord into Heaven

THE FRUIT OF THIS MYSTERY

The grace to despise the things of this world, in light of the surpassing greatness of the heavenly things to which we are called

WHEN THE LORD ASCENDED into heaven, the disciples adored Him from where His feet had previously stood, then immediately they returned to Jerusalem, where they were commanded to wait for the Promise of the

Father. Great indeed was their joy, for they rejoice that their God and Lord, after the triumph of His resurrection, has also passed into the heavens. (ST. BEDE)

OUR FATHER   Our Father, Who art in Heaven, hallowed be Thy name, Thy kingdom come, Thy will be done, on earth as it is in heaven. Give us this day our daily bread; and forgive us our trespasses, as we forgive those who trespass against us; and lead us not into temptation, but deliver us from evil. Amen.

HAIL MARY (10)   Hail Mary, Full of Grace, the Lord is with thee. Blessed art thou among women and blessed is the fruit of thy womb, Jesus. Holy Mary, Mother of God, pray for us sinners now, and at the hour of our death. Amen.

1. And so, when they were led up to the Mount of Olives, they formed a circle around the Benefactor. The Lord, raising His hands like wings, just as the eagle covers the nest of young birds which she warms, spoke to the nestlings, saying, "I have sheltered you from all evil, since I loved you and you loved Me. I will not be separated from you; I am with you." (ST. ROMANOS THE MELODIST)

2. The Lord appeared to them on the mountain to signify that the body, which at His birth He had taken of the common dust of the human race, He had, by His Resurrection, exalted above all earthly things. By this He wanted to teach the faithful that if they desire to see the height of His Resurrection, they must endeavour in this world to pass from low pleasures to high desires. (ST. BEDE)

3. Since He is sending them out among the Gentiles to face death and danger, just before His Ascension, He gives them courage by saying, "Fear not, for I will be with you until the end of the age." See also how He mentions the end so as to arouse in them disdain for these calamities. "Do not be downcast", He says, "for all things will have an end, both worldly sorrows and worldly joys. Do not be oppressed by sorrows for they will pass, and do not be deceived by good things, for they too will come to an end." His promise to be with them was not made only to the apostles, but to all His disciples, for, of course, the apostles would not live till the end. He makes this promise even to us, and to those after us. (THEOPHYLACT)

4. And because what He had commanded them to do was great, in order to exalt their spirits He adds, "And, behold, I am with you always, even unto the end of the world." As much as to say, "Do not tell Me of the difficulty of the things I command of you, seeing that I am with you, Who can make all things easy." A like promise He often made to the prophets in the Old Testament, to Jeremiah who pleaded that he was just a child, to Moses and to Ezekiel, when they would have shunned the office imposed upon them. He brings before them the end of the world, that He may the more draw them on, and that they may not look merely to present inconveniences, but to the infinite goods to come. As much as to say, "The grievous things which you shall undergo terminate with this present life, seeing that even this world shall come to an end, but the good things which you shall enjoy will endure forever." (ST. JOHN CHRYSOSTOM)

5. Elijah, according to what we read, went up to heaven in a chariot, this showed that being a man he needed outside help. Elijah, lacking as he was by the weakness of his nature, could not ascend by himself to heaven, even if it were just to the airy sky. As for our Redeemer, we do not read that He was raised by a chariot or by the angels, He, Who created everything, needed only His own power to be carried above all. He was going back to where He was already, He came back to where He lived, since even when He ascended to heaven by His humanity, He contained both the earth and heaven by His divinity. (ST. GREGORY THE GREAT)

6. At the time of our Lord's birth, the angels that appeared did not dress in white, unlike those we read of those sent during His Ascension. The white clothes manifest joy and celebration for those spirits, for the entrance into Heaven of the God made man was a great feast for the angels. If by the birth of the Lord, the Deity seemed lowered, by His Ascension, humanity was glorified. The angels dressed in the white of celebration at the moment of the Lord's ascension because the One they saw as a humbled in His birth now manifests Himself in His glory. (ST. GREGORY THE GREAT)

7. After the Resurrection, the Leader gathered together the lambs whom fear had scattered at the time of the Crucifixion, and standing on the mountain top, He sang a sweet song, giving courage to the flock. It was as though He wanted to speak words of encouragement for timid men, He said, "Be of good courage, I alone have conquered the world, I alone have scattered the wolves, no one was with Me; I was the One, the only One, and I alone know what is in the heart." (ST. ROMANOS THE MELODIST)

8. And so, dearly-beloved, let us rejoice with spiritual joy, and with gladness pay God worthy thanks and raise our minds unimpeded to those heights where Christ is. Minds that have heard the call to be uplifted must not be pressed down by earthly affections, they that are fore-ordained to things eternal must not be taken up with the things that perish, they that have entered on the way of Truth must not be entangled in treacherous snares. Each one of us must so take our course through these temporal things as to remember that we are sojourning in the vale of this world, in which, even though we meet with some attractions, we must not sinfully embrace them, but bravely pass through them. (ST. LEO THE GREAT)

9. Do you see then to what height of glory human nature has been raised? Is it not from earth to heaven? Is it not from corruption to incorruption? Indeed, Christ's human nature is worshipped in the heavens by every creature seen and unseen. And for us, although we were alienated and hostile in our intent by evil deeds, we have not only been reconciled to God the Father through our Lord Jesus Christ, but we have also soared aloft to sonship. We share His sonship, and how hard would not someone toil in order to become the intimate friend of a corruptible king here below? (ST. EPHREM)

10. And truly great and unspeakable was the joy of the apostles, when, in the sight of the holy multitude, the nature of mankind went up, passing above the angels' ranks and rising beyond the archangels', until it was received to sit with the Eternal Father, to Whose nature It was united in the Son. Christ's Ascension is our uplifting and our hope, for where the glory of the Head has gone before, we hope to join. For today, not only are we confirmed as possessors of paradise, but

have also in Christ penetrated the heights of heaven, and have gained greater things through Christ's unspeakable grace than we had lost through the devil's malice. That virulent enemy had driven us out from the bliss of our first abode, but now, the Son of God, Who had made us members of Himself, places us at the right hand of the Father, with Whom He lives and reigns in the unity of the Holy Spirit, God for ever and ever. (ST. LEO THE GREAT)

GLORY BE TO THE FATHER   Glory be to the Father, and to the Son, and to the Holy Spirit, as it was in the beginning, is now and ever shall be, world without end. Amen.

THE FATIMA PRAYER   O my Jesus, forgive us our sins, save us from the fires of hell, lead all souls to heaven, especially those in most need of Thy mercy.

The Descent of the Holy Spirit on Our Lady and the Apostles

THE FRUIT OF THIS MYSTERY

That the sanctification through the indwelling of the Holy Spirit may impel us to convert all people to the Holy Catholic Faith

"AND THEY WERE ALL filled with the Holy Spirit, and began to speak with other tongues, as the Holy Spirit gave them utterance." How swift are the words of wisdom, and where God is the Master, how quickly is what is

89

taught learnt. No interpretation is required for understanding, no practice for using, no time for studying, but the Spirit of Truth blowing where He wills, makes the languages peculiar to each nation the common property in the mouth of the Church. And therefore from that day the trumpet of the Gospel preaching has sounded loud, from that day the showers of gracious gifts, the rivers of blessings, have watered every desert and all the dry land. (ST. LEO THE GREAT)

OUR FATHER   Our Father, Who art in Heaven, hallowed be Thy name, Thy kingdom come, Thy will be done, on earth as it is in heaven. Give us this day our daily bread; and forgive us our trespasses, as we forgive those who trespass against us; and lead us not into temptation, but deliver us from evil. Amen.

HAIL MARY (10)   Hail Mary, Full of Grace, the Lord is with thee. Blessed art thou among women and blessed is the fruit of thy womb, Jesus. Holy Mary, Mother of God, pray for us sinners now, and at the hour of our death. Amen.

1. The Holy Ghost didn't come to them while Christ was with them or even immediately after His departure, but rather on the day of Pentecost. It was fitting that they should first be brought to have a longing desire for that event, and so receive the grace. For this reason Christ Himself departed, and then the Spirit descended. For had He been been there Himself they would not have expected the Spirit as earnestly as they did. On this account neither did He come immediately after Christ's Ascension, but after eight or nine days. It is the same with us also, for our desires towards God are most raised when we most stand in need. We are often made to wait that we might might first feel despondent for a while, and be made,

as I said, to feel our need of Him. Then after He comes we reap a full and unalloyed delight. (ST. JOHN CHRYSOSTOM)

2. Jesus tells His holy disciples that they will be more courageous and understand better once they are endowed with power from on high, and that when their minds are illuminated by the torch of the Spirit they will be able to see into all things, even though they will no longer be able to question Him through His bodily presence among them. The Saviour does not say that they will no longer need the light of His guidance, but that when they have received His Spirit, when He is dwelling in their hearts, they will not be wanting in any good thing, and their minds will be filled with most perfect knowledge. (ST. CYRIL OF ALEXANDRIA)

3. "After His Ascension, the holy mother of Christ was the model and leader of every good activity for men and for women through the grace and support of her glorious king and son. And that is why she then instructed the holy apostles in fasting and prayer, and they were devoted to fasting and prayer and supplication until the fiftieth day was completed, and they were filled with the grace of the comforting Holy Spirit." * (ST. MAXIMUS THE CONFESSOR)

4. If we are not to be scorched and made unfruitful, we need the dew of God. Since we have our accuser, we need an Advocate as well. And so the Lord in His pity for man, who had fallen into the hands of brigands, having Himself bound up

---

* Maximus the Confessor, *"The Life of the Virgin",* (Yale: Bloomsbury 2012), 121.

his wounds and left for his care two coins bearing the royal image, entrusted him to the Holy Spirit. Now, through the Spirit, the image and inscription of the Father and the Son have been given to us, and it is our duty to use the coins committed to our charge and make them yield a rich profit for the Lord. (ST. IRENAEUS)

5. "And My Father will love him, and We will come to him and make Our home with him." My friends, consider the greatness of this solemn feast that commemorates God's coming as a guest into our hearts! If some rich and influential friend were to come to your home, you would promptly put it all in order for fear something there might offend your friend's eyes when he came in. Let all of us then, who are preparing our inner homes for God, cleanse them of everything our wrongdoing has brought into them. (ST. GREGORY THE GREAT)

6. And therefore He came after Christ, that a Comforter should not be lacking to us, "another Comforter", showing His co-equality with Christ and His equal Lordship. The Spirit came in the form of tongues because of His close relation to the Word. And the tongues were of Fire, perhaps because of His purifying power or else to remind us that Our God is a consuming Fire, and a Fire burning up the ungodly. (ST. GREGORY NAZIENZAN)

7. This is the same Holy Spirit by Whom love is poured into our hearts. It was love that was to bring the Church of God together all over the world. And as individual men who received the Holy Spirit in those days could speak in all kinds of tongues, so today the Church, united by the Holy Spirit, speaks in the language of every people. I, belonging to the

body of Christ, that is, the Church, share in this same gift. For what else did the presence of the Holy Spirit indicate at Pentecost, except that God's Church was to speak in the language of every people? By this spectacular miracle they became a sign of the Catholic Church, which embraces the language of every nation. Keep this feast, then, as members of the one body of Christ. This Church is the house of God, built up of living stones, whose master is Almighty God. It is His delight to dwell here. (SIXTH CENTURY, NORTH AFRICAN THEOLOGIAN)

8. St. John took the Virgin into his house till the day of her death, and he ministered to her in all the assistance that she needed and he obeyed her as a servant obeying his master. And she, the holy Virgin, loved him as a mother loves her children. She worked many cures like those of her beloved Son Jesus Christ our Lord, but she would not allow the apostles to write them, because she fled from all unnecessary glory in the sight of men. The apostles always followed her, and were taught by her the preaching of the Gospel. (FIFTH CENTURY, SAHIDIC SERMON FRAGMENTS)

9. Blessed are You, O Christ our God, the One Who has now manifested the fishermen as most wise through the sending down of the Holy Spirit upon them. Through them You drew the world into Your net, O Lover of man, glory to You! (EIGHTH CENTURY, BYZANTINE LITURGY)

10. And so, under the influence of heavenly power, and with the divine co-operation, the doctrine of the Saviour, like the rays of the sun, quickly illumined the whole world and straight away, in accordance with the divine Scriptures, the voice of

the inspired evangelists and apostles went forth through all the earth, and their words to the end of the world. In every city and village, churches were quickly established, filled with multitudes of people like a replenished threshing-floor. And those whose minds, in consequence of errors which had descended to them from their forefathers, were fettered by the ancient disease of idolatrous superstition, were, by the power of Christ operating through the teaching and the wonderful works of His disciples, set free, as it were, from terrible masters, and found a release from the most cruel bondage. (EUSEBIUS OF CAESAREA)

GLORY BE TO THE FATHER   Glory be to the Father, and to the Son, and to the Holy Spirit, as it was in the beginning, is now and ever shall be, world without end. Amen.

THE FATIMA PRAYER   O my Jesus, forgive us our sins, save us from the fires of hell, lead all souls to heaven, especially those in most need of Thy mercy.

The Assumption of the Blessed Virgin Mary, Body and Soul, into Heaven

THE FRUIT OF THIS MYSTERY

A tender love and devotion towards Our Blessed Mother

THE HOLY APOSTLES WERE gathered together, caught up even by clouds and taken from the ends of the earth, so that they might be assembled as a group. The glorious Twelve and many others who followed them came to glorify the holy and glorious mother of the Lord.

And the mystery of the second coming was made manifest here. (FIFTH CENTURY, PSEUDO JOHN THE THEOLOGIAN)

OUR FATHER   Our Father, Who art in Heaven, hallowed be Thy name, Thy kingdom come, Thy will be done, on earth as it is in heaven. Give us this day our daily bread; and forgive us our trespasses, as we forgive those who trespass against us; and lead us not into temptation, but deliver us from evil. Amen.

HAIL MARY (10)   Hail Mary, Full of Grace, the Lord is with thee. Blessed art thou among women and blessed is the fruit of thy womb, Jesus. Holy Mary, Mother of God, pray for us sinners now, and at the hour of our death. Amen.

1. Our Lady returned to visit Bethlehem, having with her three virgins who ministered to her. And after having rested a short time, she sat up and said to the virgins, "Bring me some burning incense, that I may pray", and they brought it, and then she prayed, saying, "My Lord Jesus Christ, Who deigned through Your supreme goodness to be born of me, hear my voice, and send me Your apostle John, in order that, seeing him, I may partake of joy, and send me also the rest of Your apostles, in whatever country they may be, in order that, having beheld them, I may bless Your name much to be praised, for I am confident that You hear Your servant in everything." (FIFTH CENTURY, PSEUDO JOHN THE THEOLOGIAN)

2. Now, it came to pass that fifteen years after the Lord rose from the dead, one day, the holy Virgin Mary called to John, and said to him, "Fetch for me Peter and James, and let them come to me." And he ran in haste, and called them to her. When therefore they arrived, the three sat by her and the

Fountain of the Water of Life opened her mouth, and said to them, "Hear me, O apostles, you who the Lord chose for Himself to preach the gospel of the Kingdom of Heaven in all the world. Do not grieve in your heart at that which I will tell you now. For behold, the time of my departure is near at hand, that I shall lay down my body and that my soul and my spirit may go to the Lord, to enjoy the good things which God has prepared for those who love Him." (FIFTH CENTURY, SAHIDIC SERMON FRAGMENTS)

3. When the day of her departure had come, the holy Mother of God called John and said to him, "Arise, light lamps and torches, for evening has come." And she took some linen cloths and spread them on the ground like a bed or a couch, and poured out perfumes upon them. She turned to the apostles and said to them, "Let us pray to God the merciful to have mercy on us." And so she turned her face eastwards, and prayed, saying, "I thank You God the Father Almighty, I thank You only begotten Son Who came into the world to save all souls, I thank You Holy Spirit, Who came upon me, and Your holy power that overshadowed me. Now therefore, my Lord and my God, the hour has come for You to come unto me and have mercy on me, and remove from me this world. Let those that are on Your left hand fall before me, and those on the right stand up with joy. Let all the powers of darkness be ashamed today, because they have found nothing of theirs in me. Open to me the gates of righteousness, that I may enter into them, and be manifested to the face of my God." (FIFTH CENTURY, SAHIDIC SERMON FRAGMENTS)

4. What, then, shall we call this mystery of yours? Death? Your blessed soul is naturally parted from your blissful and

undefiled body, and the body is delivered to the grave, yet it does not remain in death, nor is it the prey of corruption. The body of her, whose virginity remained unspotted in child-birth, was preserved in its incorruption, and was taken to a better, diviner place, where death is not, but eternal life. Therefore I will not call your sacred transformation death, but rest or going home, and it is more truly a going home. Putting off corporeal things, you dwell now in a happier state. How could Limbo open its gates to her? How could corruption touch the life-giving body? These are things quite foreign to the soul and body of God's Mother. Death trembled before her. In approaching her Son, death had learnt experience from His sufferings and had grown wiser. The gloomy descent to hell was not for her, but a joyous, easy, and sweet passage to heaven. (ST. JOHN DAMASCENE)

5. What countless angels acclaim the death of the life-giving Mother! How the eloquence of apostles blesses the departure of this body which was the receptacle of God. How the Word of God, Who deigned in His mercy to become her Son, receives the holy soul of His mother. We may well believe that the angelic choirs waited to receive your departing soul. O what a blessed departure was yours as you went to be with your God. (ST. JOHN DAMASCENE)

6. Nature, I conjecture, is stirred to its depths, strange sounds and voices are heard, and the swelling hymns of angels who precede, accompany, and follow her. Some constitute the guard of honour to that undefiled and immaculate soul on its way to heaven until the queen reaches the divine throne. Others surrounding the sacred and divine body proclaim God's mother in angelic harmony. What of those who watched

by the most holy and immaculate body? In loving reverence and with tears of joy they gathered round the blessed and divine tabernacle, embracing every member, and were filled with holiness and thanksgiving. Then illnesses were cured, and demons were put to flight and banished to the regions of darkness. The air and atmosphere and heavens were sanctified by her passage through them, the earth by the burial of her body. Nor was water deprived of a blessing. She was washed in pure water. It did not cleanse her, but was rather itself sanctified. Then, hearing was given to the deaf, the lame recovered their feet and the blind their sight. Sinners who approached with faith blotted out the hand-writing against them. Then the holy body is wrapped in a snow-white winding sheet, and the queen is again laid upon her bed. Then follow lights and incense and hymns, and angels singing as befits the solemnity; apostles and patriarchs acclaiming her in inspired song. (ST. JOHN DAMASCENE)

7. Then the Saviour ordered the archangel Michael to roll back the stone from the door of the tomb; and the Lord said, "Arise, My beloved and My nearest relation, the one who has not put on corruption by relations with man, I forbid you to suffer destruction of your body in the sepulchre." And immediately Mary rose from the tomb, and blessed the Lord, and falling forward at the feet of the Lord, adored Him, saying, "I cannot render sufficient thanks to You, O Lord, for Your boundless benefits which You have deigned to bestow upon me Your handmaiden." Together they were lifted up on a cloud, and taken back into heaven, and the angels along with them. The Lord Jesus led the blessed Mary into the paradise of God. (FIFTH CENTURY, PSEUDO JOHN THE THEOLOGIAN)

8. "When on this day the glorious Virgin ascended into heaven, undoubtedly, she filled to overflowing the joy of the heavenly citizens. For it was the Virgin, at whose voice the very babes, still shut up in their mothers' wombs, leapt for joy. If the soul of a tiny babe not yet born melted with joy as Mary spoke, how unimaginably greater must have been the joy in heaven among those who were found worthy to hear her voice, and to see her face, and to rejoice in her blessed presence? But who can conceive the wonder of this day's procession, the glorious Queen of the world, with the whole army of the heavenly legions going forth to meet her, and conducting her with songs and canticles to her throne of glory, where her Son receives and embraces her, with a peaceful countenance and a graceful manner, and exalts her above every creature, giving her the honor due to such a Mother with the glory that behooves such a Son? Altogether lovely were the kisses of the lips of the Babe at the breast, and they gave gladness to his Mother when he lay in her virginal breast. Must we not think those to be sweeter far which she receives from His lips in welcome as He sits on the right hand of his Father, and as she ascends to her throne of glory, singing her marriage song, and crying, "Let Him kiss me with the kisses of His mouth?" Who shall declare the generation of Christ and the assumption of Mary? For as on earth she was found more full of grace than all other creatures, so in heaven she attains to a unique glory." (ST. BERNARD)

9. The most blessed Thomas came past the Mount of Olives and he saw the most blessed body going up to heaven and he began to cry out and say, "O Holy Mother, Blessed Mother, Spotless Mother, if I have now found grace because I see you, make your servant joyful through your compassion, because

you are going to heaven." Then the girdle with which the apostles had encircled her most holy body was thrown down from heaven to the blessed Thomas. And taking it, and kissing it, and giving thanks to God, he came again into the Valley of Jehoshaphat. He found all the apostles and another great crowd there beating their breasts on account of the brightness which they had seen. Blessed Thomas asked them, "Where have you laid her body?" And they pointed out the sepulchre with their finger. And he said, "The body which is called most holy is not there." Then they all went to the sepulchre, but they did not find the body, and they did not know what to say, because they had been convicted by the words of Thomas. Then the blessed Thomas told them how he was singing mass in India, he still had on his sacerdotal robes, and from there he had been brought to the Mount of Olives, and had seen the most holy body of the blessed Mary going up into heaven, and how she had thrown him the girdle which she had been wearing. (FIFTH CENTURY, PSEUDO JOHN THE THEOLOGIAN)

10. And the same cloud by which they had been brought carried them back, each to his own place, just like Philip when he baptised the eunuch, or Habakkuk, who was carried by the Spirit to Daniel in the lions' den. And so the apostles quickly returned to where they had at first been, to preach to the people of God. Nor is it to be wondered that God should do such things, He, Who went into the Virgin and came out of her though her womb was closed. The Holy Spirit continued working through the disciples, who made the deaf to hear, raised the dead, cleansed the lepers, gave sight to the blind, and did many other wonderful things. To believe this is no doubtful matter. (FIFTH CENTURY, PSEUDO JOHN THE THEOLOGIAN)

GLORY BE TO THE FATHER   Glory be to the Father, and to the Son, and to the Holy Spirit, as it was in the beginning, is now and ever shall be, world without end. Amen.

THE FATIMA PRAYER   O my Jesus, forgive us our sins, save us from the fires of hell, lead all souls to heaven, especially those in most need of Thy mercy.

The Coronation of the Virgin
Mary as Queen of Heaven

THE FRUIT OF THIS MYSTERY

*A continual dependence on Our Lady as Mediatrix of All Graces
and a desire to make this Queenship known to all men*

THE LORD HAD PREVIOUSLY told His mother, "I will come for you, and I will take your soul and your spirit into My spiritual city, the heavenly Jerusalem. All My holy ones shall wonder at the great glory which I will give you there through My good Father, and You shall be exalted above all the holy ones, for you are the glory of their strength. I will cause My angels to keep singing your praises for ever, for you are like them in your holiness and your purity. All the ranks of the heavens will rejoice at your coming to them. The patriarchs and the prophets shall come forth to meet you, they will rejoice in your presence, saying, "Behold the Mother of our Life has come to us." (FIFTH CENTURY, SAHIDIC SERMON FRAGMENTS)

OUR FATHER   Our Father, Who art in Heaven, hallowed be Thy name, Thy kingdom come, Thy will be done, on earth as it is in heaven. Give us this day our daily bread; and forgive us our trespasses, as we forgive those who trespass against us; and lead us not into temptation, but deliver us from evil. Amen.

HAIL MARY (10)   Hail Mary, Full of Grace, the Lord is with thee. Blessed art thou among women and blessed is the fruit of thy womb, Jesus. Holy Mary, Mother of God, pray for us sinners now, and at the hour of our death. Amen.

1. Straight away we looked and saw a great chariot of light. It came and stayed in our midst, there were cherubim drawing it, the holy Virgin Mary sitting upon it, and shining ten thousand times more than the sun and the moon. And we were in fear and fell on our face and revered her, and she stretched forth her hand towards us all, and blessed us, and gave us the salutation of peace. Again we praised her, being in great joy and exultation, and she told us great and hidden mysteries, which it is not lawful to manifest because of men that are unfaithful. And the Lord called into the tomb and raised the body of His virgin mother, and put her soul into

her body again, and we saw it living in the body even as it was with us formerly, wearing the flesh. And our Saviour stretched out His hand and set her on the chariot with Him. And our Saviour said to us in His gentle voice, "Behold My beloved mother." (SIXTH CENTURY, BOHAIRIC SERMON FRAGMENTS)

2. Peter and John looked at her, as she flew to the heavens. And all the while singing before her were ten thousand times ten thousand of angels, it seemed a crowd without number. And the apostles did not leave standing and looking at the body of the Virgin until the angels were hidden with her, once again, in the air. Thus the Queen and mother of the King arose into the heavens. (FIFTH CENTURY, SAHIDIC SERMON FRAGMENTS)

3. What shall we say, O Queen? What words shall we use? What praise shall we pour upon your sacred and glorified head, O giver of good gifts and of riches, the pride of the human race, the glory of all creation, through whom it is truly blessed. He Whom nature did not contain in the beginning, was born of you. The Invisible One is contemplated face to face. O Word of God, open my slow lips, and give their utterances Your richest blessing; inflame me with the grace of Your Spirit, through Whom fishermen became orators, and ignorant men spoke supernatural wisdom, so that my feeble voices may contribute to Your Beloved Mother's praises. (ST. JOHN DAMASCENE)

4. Angels with archangels bear you up. Impure spirits trembled at your departure. The air raises a hymn of praise at your passage, and the atmosphere is purified. Heaven receives your soul with joy. The heavenly powers greet you with sacred

canticles and with joyous praise, saying, "Who is this most pure creature ascending, shining as the dawn, beautiful as the moon, conspicuous as the sun? How sweet and lovely you are, the lily of the field, the rose among thorns." (ST. JOHN DAMASCENE)

5. The King introduces you into His chamber. There Powers protect you, Principalities praise you, Thrones proclaim you, Cherubim are hushed in joy and Seraphim magnify the true Mother of their very Lord. You were not taken into heaven as Elijah was, nor did you penetrate to the third heaven with Paul, but you have reached the royal throne of your Son, seeing it with your own eyes, standing by it in joy and unspeakable familiarity. O gladness of angels and of all heavenly powers, sweetness of patriarchs and of the just, perpetual exultation of prophets, rejoicing the world and sanctifying all things, refreshment of the weary, comfort of the sorrowful, remission of sins, health of the sick, harbour of the storm-tossed, lasting strength of mourners and perpetual succour of all who invoke you. (ST. JOHN DAMASCENE)

6. This body shall be raised, not remaining weak as it is now, but this same body shall be raised. By putting on incorruption, it shall be altered, as iron blending with fire becomes fire, or rather, in a manner the Lord Who raises us knows. However it will be, this body shall be raised, but it shall not remain such as it is. Rather, it shall abide as an eternal body. It shall no longer require for its life such nourishment as now, nor shall it require a ladder for its ascent; for it shall be made a spiritual body, a marvellous thing, such as we have not the ability to describe. (CYRIL OF JERUSALEM)

7. You, Mother, are close to everyone and protect everyone, and even though our eyes cannot see you, we know that you live in the midst of all of us and that you make yourself present in the most varied of ways. You are the one who appears in beauty, and your virginal body is all holy, all chaste, entirely the dwelling place of God and exempt from dissolution into dust. Though still human, your body is changed into the heavenly life of incorruptibility, truly living and glorious, undamaged and sharing in perfect life. (ST. GERMANUS OF CONSTANTINOPLE)

8. In dangers, in doubts, in difficulties, think of Mary, call upon Mary. Let not her name depart from your lips, never suffer it to leave your heart. And that you may obtain the assistance of her prayer, neglect not to walk in her footsteps. With her for guide, you shall never go astray. While invoking her, you shall never lose heart. So long as she is in your mind, you are safe from deception. While she holds your hand, you cannot fall, under her protection you have nothing to fear. If she walks before you, you shall not grow weary, if she shows you favour, you shall reach the goal. (ST. BERNARD)

9. O Maiden, empress and ruler, queen and lady, protect and keep me in your arms so that Satan, the evil-doer, is unable to rise up against me, so that my wicked foe may never have any triumph over me. (ST. EPHREM)

10. Blessed Virgin Mary, who can worthily repay you with praise and thanksgiving for having rescued a fallen world by your generous consent? Accept then such poor thanks as we have to offer, unequal though they may be to your merits.

Receive our gratitude and obtain by your prayers the pardon of our sins. Take our prayers into the sanctuary of heaven and enable them to bring about our peace with God. Holy Mary, help the miserable, strengthen the discouraged, comfort the sorrowful, pray for your people, plead for the clergy, intercede for all women consecrated to God. May all who venerate you, feel now your help and protection. Make it your continual care to pray for the people of God, for you were blessed by God and were made worthy to bear the Redeemer of the world, Who lives and reigns for ever. (ST AUGUSTINE)

GLORY BE TO THE FATHER   Glory be to the Father, and to the Son, and to the Holy Spirit, as it was in the beginning, is now and ever shall be, world without end. Amen.

THE FATIMA PRAYER   O my Jesus, forgive us our sins, save us from the fires of hell, lead all souls to heaven, especially those in most need of Thy mercy.

CONCLUDING PRAYERS   *Upon completing the recitation of the Holy Rosary, the following prayers are customary, but others too may be added according to one's devotion and preference.*

HAIL HOLY QUEEN PRAYER   Hail Holy Queen, Mother of Mercy, hail our life, our sweetness and our hope. To thee do we cry, poor banished children of Eve, to thee do we send up our sighs, mourning and weeping in this vale of tears. Turn then, most gracious advocate, thine eyes of mercy towards us, and after this, our exile, show unto us the blessed fruit of thy womb, Jesus. O clement, O loving, O sweet Virgin Mary. Pray for us O holy Mother of God, that we may be made worthy of the promises of Christ.

Let Us Pray O God, Whose only begotten son, by His life, death and resurrection, has purchased for us the rewards of eternal life, grant we beseech Thee, that meditating on these mysteries of the most Holy Rosary of the Blessed Virgin Mary, we may both imitate what they contain and obtain what they promise, through the same Christ our Lord. Amen.

SAINT MICHAEL THE ARCHANGEL PRAYER Holy Michael, the Archangel, defend us in the day of battle. Be our safeguard against the wickedness and snares of the devil. May God rebuke him, we humbly pray; and do thou, O Prince of the heavenly hosts, by the power of God thrust down into hell Satan and all the evil spirits who wander through the world seeking the ruin of souls. Amen.

MEMORARE PRAYER Remember, O most gracious Virgin Mary, that never was it known that anyone who fled to thy protection, implored thy help, or sought thine intercession was left unaided. Inspired by this confidence, I fly unto thee, O Virgin of virgins, my mother; to thee do I come, before thee I stand, sinful and sorrowful. O Mother of the Word Incarnate, despise not my petitions, but in thy mercy hear and answer me. Amen.

May the Divine Assistance remain always with us, and may the souls of the faithful departed, through the mercy of God rest in peace. Amen.

The Mysteries of Light

The Baptism of Christ in the River Jordan

THE FRUIT OF THIS MYSTERY

A greater joy in recognising the friendship with God that is open to us through the Sacrament of Baptism

AT CHRIST'S BAPTISM THE Father proclaimed the Son, the Holy Spirit came likewise and brought the same voice upon the head of Christ, in order that no one present might think that what was being said of Christ, was said of John. How then did the Jews fail to believe having received such a vision? Understanding such sights requires more than bodily vision, just as those who saw the miracles of Christ were so drunken with malice that they denied what their own eyes had seen. For such men even the appearance of the Holy Spirit in the form of a dove failed to overcome their incredulity. Only by John, and the more devout number of the people, was the vision understood. Even so, John does not fail to repeat to them the things he has seen, adding, "I saw, and I bear witness that this is the Son of God." (ST. JOHN CHRYSOSTOM)

OUR FATHER   Our Father, Who art in Heaven, hallowed be Thy name, Thy kingdom come, Thy will be done, on earth as it is in heaven. Give us this day our daily bread; and forgive us our trespasses, as we forgive those who trespass against us; and lead us not into temptation, but deliver us from evil. Amen.

HAIL MARY (10)   Hail Mary, Full of Grace, the Lord is with thee. Blessed art thou among women and blessed is the fruit of thy womb, Jesus. Holy Mary, Mother of God, pray for us sinners now, and at the hour of our death. Amen.

1. John entered this world in the spirit and power of Elijah, and from childhood remained removed from the society of men. This great prophet stayed in the wilderness, in uninterrupted contemplation of invisible things. To what height of divine grace was he raised! Greater favour was bestowed upon him than all the prophets, such that from the beginning of his life even to the end he always presented his heart before

God in utmost purity and free from every fallen passion. (ST. GREGORY OF NYSSA)

2. John wore clothes made of camel hair, a garment not soft and delicate, but hairy, heavy and rough. It was something to wound the skin rather than comfort it. See how even the very clothing of his body told of the virtue of his mind. Compared with the holiness of John, who is there that can think himself righteous? As a white garment, if placed near snow, would seem foul by the contrast, so compared with John every man would seem impure. For that reason a great crowd came and confessed their sins before him. A God fearing man will be quick to wish to make a confession of his sins, for fear takes away all shame. But even if we do still feel shame, confession is good and God bids us to do so. Let the shame be taken as a punishment for the sin. (FIFTH CENTURY, PSEUDO CHRYSOSTOM)

3. I saw John, filled with astonishment, with crowds standing round him while the glorious Bridegroom bent down before the child of barren parents to be baptised. My mind was amazed at both Word and Voice, John was the Voice, our Lord, Who shone forth, was like the Word ready to come out into the open, having been hidden. It was then that the Groom revealed Himself, coming to John by the river. The herald trembled as he announced, "Here is the Groom Whom I have been proclaiming." (FIFTH CENTURY, SYRIAC DIALOGUE HYMN)

4. There came to baptism He who baptises all, manifesting Himself by the Jordan. John beheld Him and withdrew his hand, using words of supplication, as follows, "How is it,

Lord, that You should be baptised, for at Your baptism You bring forgiveness to all. The font looks expectantly towards You, sprinkle in it sanctification and it will be perfected." Our Lord spoke, "I have willed it, approach and baptise Me, that My will may be done. Draw near and baptise Me, you will not get burnt. The bridal chamber is ready, do not hold Me back from the wedding feast that lies prepared. I will be baptised while the crowd look on, for the Father Who sent Me will testify that I am His Son in Whom He is well pleased. O Voice crying in the wilderness, perform the task for which you came, so that the wilderness, to which you set out, may wonder at the fulfilment of all you have proclaimed." (FIFTH CENTURY, SYRIAC DIALOGUE HYMN)

5. So the Lord was baptised, He did not go to be purified but to purify the waters, so that, washed by the sinless flesh of Christ, they might have the power to baptise. So whoever comes to the bath of Christ can leave his sins there. Christ washes us in His body. He came down so that we all might be brought up. He took upon Himself the sins of all, so that in Him the sins of all might be cleansed. If for us Christ washed Himself, how much more must we wash our faults! "Purify yourself," as the apostle says, "for Christ purified Himself for us, the One Who did not need purification." (ST. AMBROSE)

6. The Lord Jesus is baptised not as Himself requiring purification but in order to make my purification His own. He does this so that He might break the head of the dragon in the water, that He might wash away sin and bury the old Adam in the water, that He might sanctify the Baptist, that He might fulfil the Law, that He might reveal the mystery of the Trinity and that He might become the type and example

to us of baptism. We are baptised in the one perfect baptism of our Lord, the baptism of water and the Holy Spirit. (ST. JOHN DAMASCENE)

7. John then calls Christ the Lamb of God, because God the Father had accepted His death for our salvation, and because He Himself willed this for our sakes. And whereas the lambs of the Old Testament could not take away sin, this One alone has taken away the sin of the whole world, rescuing it from the danger it was in from the wrath of God. Notice how John says "Who takes away" and not "Who will take away", for the Lord Jesus did not only take away our sins when He suffered, but from that time even to the present He lives to takes away our sins. Jesus is ever desirous to take away our sins by means of His one perfect sacrifice on the cross. (THEOPHYLACT)

8. John does not make a long discourse, he has only one object before him, to bring all those around him to Christ, knowing that then they will no longer need his witness. John proclaims this publicly, in the presence of all. John does not exhort, he simply gazes in admiration at Christ, pointing out the gift He came to bestow, the cleansing from sin, and the mode in which He would accomplish it, though being the Lamb of God. Two of John's disciples who stood nearby undertook to follow Christ, and from then on they remained firm in following Him. (ST. JOHN CHRYSOSTOM)

9. And besides following Christ, their questions show their love for Him, calling Him "Master" before they had even learnt anything from Him, and then they ask, "Where do You live?" In response, Christ does not merely tell them where to

find His house, but brings the two disciples with Him, showing that He has already accepted them as His own. He doesn't say, "It is not the time now, come back tomorrow if you wish to learn form Me", instead, He addresses them familiarly, as if they were friends who had lived with Him a long time. And what a strong desire they had to hear Him! For they didn't leave Him even at sunset. (ST. JOHN CHRYSOSTOM)

10. He showed the two disciples the place where He dwelt and they came and remained with Him. What a blessed day they spent, what a blessed night! Who can make known to us those things which they heard from the Lord? Let us also build in our heart, and make a house into which He may come and teach us, and converse with us. Do not love God for the sake of a reward, let Him be the reward. Let your soul say, "One thing have I desired of the Lord, that will I seek after, that I may dwell in the house of the Lord all the days of my life, that I may behold the beauty of the Lord." This beauty will ever be present to you, and you shall never be satisfied; indeed you shall be always satisfied, and yet never satisfied. (ST. AUGUSTINE)

GLORY BE TO THE FATHER   Glory be to the Father, and to the Son, and to the Holy Spirit, as it was in the beginning, is now and ever shall be, world without end. Amen.

THE FATIMA PRAYER   O my Jesus, forgive us our sins, save us from the fires of hell, lead all souls to heaven, especially those in most need of Thy mercy.

The Wedding feast of Cana

THE FRUIT OF THIS MYSTERY

*Confidence in the power of Our Lord to work miracles, and His sovereign
willingness to work them through the intercession of His holy mother*

WHEN THE WINE RAN out at the wedding, Mary was
assured that Jesus would not grieve her in anything
that she might ask of Him, and so she approached
the place whereon her son was reclining with utmost reverence. The Virgin said, "My son, my beloved, the One Who
my soul desires, my Lord and my God! I beg you to manifest

Your power as Son of God. Let all the nations know that You are the Christ, the Son of the living God. For my son, they have no wine." And Jesus said to His mother in a kindly voice, "Woman, what do you wish with Me? My hour is not yet come." But His mother, being assured that He would not grieve her in anything, spoke to the ones who were serving and said, "Whatever He says to you, do it." Under the Lord's instruction they hastened and filled the water-jars with water, and they brought them to Jesus, Who made the sign of the cross over the water-jars, and immediately the water was transformed into excellent wine. (FIFTH CENTURY, SAHIDIC SERMON FRAGMENTS)

OUR FATHER   Our Father, Who art in Heaven, hallowed be Thy name, Thy kingdom come, Thy will be done, on earth as it is in heaven. Give us this day our daily bread; and forgive us our trespasses, as we forgive those who trespass against us; and lead us not into temptation, but deliver us from evil. Amen.

HAIL MARY (10)   Hail Mary, Full of Grace, the Lord is with thee. Blessed art thou among women and blessed is the fruit of thy womb, Jesus. Holy Mary, Mother of God, pray for us sinners now, and at the hour of our death. Amen.

1. What marvel that Our Lord went to that house for the sake of a marriage, because had He not come into the world for the sake of a marriage? He came for His spouse, Whom He redeemed with His own blood, to whom He gave the pledge of the Spirit, and Whom He united to Himself in the womb of the Virgin. For the Word is the Bridegroom, and human flesh the bride, and both together are one Son of God and

Son of Man. That womb of the Virgin Mary is His chamber, from which He went forth as a bridegroom. What marvel then that Our Lord went to that house for a marriage, Who came to this world for a marriage. (ST. AUGUSTINE)

2. There is a mysterious allusion in the fact that the marriage is related as taking place on the third day. The third day represents the third era of the world's history, the first being the age of the patriarchs and the second the age of the prophets. The third age is the age of grace in which the Lord has now appeared in the flesh. The name of the place too where the marriage was held is not without significance, for Cana means "desire of migrating". Here we are reminded that those who are most worthy of Christ burn with devotional desire, have journeyed from from vice to virtue and desire to pass from earthly to eternal things. It is here at Cana that the wine was made to fail but it did so to give Our Lord the opportunity of bringing something even better. He manifested the glory of His divinity openly, showing that the era of grace had arrived. (ST. BEDE)

3. They invite Our Lord to the marriage, not as a great person, but merely as one they knew, one of the many. As they invited the mother, so they invited the Son, and Jesus took with Him His disciples. He came then caring more for our good than His own dignity. He Who did not shrink from taking upon Himself the form of a servant, disdained not to be considered as a mere guest at the marriage of His servants. (ST. JOHN CHRYSOSTOM)

4. A marriage feast is being held within a holy Jewish family. The Mother of the Saviour is present, and He Himself has also been invited and for that reason comes with His own disciples. He comes to work miracles rather than to feast with the others, and even more to sanctify the very beginning of the birth of man according to the flesh. For it was fitting that He, Who was renewing the very nature of man, and refashioning it all for the better, should not only impart His blessing to those already called into being, but also bless marriage and that union from which children enter this world. (ST. CYRIL OF ALEXANDRIA)

5. The Lord comes with His disciples to the marriage. The lovers of miracles had to be present with the Wonder Worker, so that they might collect the deeds He accomplished as a kind of food to their faith. When the wine ran out at the feast, His mother called the Lord Whom she knew to be a Good Lord, filled with love for men, and so she said, "They have no wine." She knew that it was in His Power to do whatsoever He wanted, and so she urges Him to the miracle. (ST. CYRIL OF ALEXANDRIA)

6. Although He had said, "My hour is not yet come", He afterwards did what His mother asked Him in order to show plainly that He was not under subjection to 'the hour'. For if He was, how could He have done this miracle before the hour appointed for it? Furthermore, He wished to show honour to His mother, and to make it clear that He did not wish to go against her. He would not put her to shame in the presence of so many, especially as she had sent the servants to Him, that the petition might come from a number, and not

from herself only, indeed, His mother said to the servants, "Whatsoever He says to you, do it." (ST. JOHN CHRYSOSTOM)

7. The Gospel makes it clear that the jars had not been used previously to hold wine, so let no unbeliever suspect that a very thin wine was made by pouring water upon dregs. Furthermore, Jesus did not draw out the new wine Himself, but ordered the servants to do so, providing witnesses of the miracle. Christ not only made wine, but the best wine. The effects of the miracles of Christ are more beautiful and better than the productions of nature. (ST. JOHN CHRYSOSTOM)

8. And then Jesus changed the water into wine, and both then and now He does not ceases to do a similar work through changing weak and unstable wills. For there are men who are very much like water, cold, weak and unsettled. O Lord, change their wills to the quality of wine, so that they be no longer washy, but have body, and be the cause of gladness in themselves and others. Who are such lukewarm ones? They are those who give their minds to the fleeting things of this present life, who fail to despise this world's luxury and who love glory and authority. All these things are like flowing waters, never stable, but ever rushing violently down the steep. The rich today is poor tomorrow, and he who one day appears with numerous attendants and many possessions is next often seen as an inhabitant of the dungeon. (ST. JOHN CHRYSOSTOM)

9. This 'miracle' of the Lord turning water into wine does not perhaps seem a 'miracle' for those who know the God Who worked it. Remember how the Same God Who on that

day filled wine in the water jars, every year makes the grape juice in our vines, something that happens so regularly that we barely think of it, and yet it is still the working of God. It is the extraordinary acts that God keeps in store for certain occasions that we notice and which we call 'miracles'. May such wonders ever rouse us out of our lethargy and bring us to worship Him, as it did for those at the wedding feast, "The Lord's glory was manifested and His disciples believed in Him." (ST. AUGUSTINE)

10. "But the water's change into wine also effected a change in the one who was the host. The bridegroom left the wedding and his home, and he followed and served the excellent guest, the gracious Lord and king and the bridegroom of immaculate and holy souls. So also the bride served the all-holy mother of the Lord, so that the miracle done by the Lord not only turned water into wine, but it also changed marriage into virginity." * (ST. MAXIMUS THE CONFESSOR)

GLORY BE TO THE FATHER   Glory be to the Father, and to the Son, and to the Holy Spirit, as it was in the beginning, is now and ever shall be, world without end. Amen.

THE FATIMA PRAYER   O my Jesus, forgive us our sins, save us from the fires of hell, lead all souls to heaven, especially those in most need of Thy mercy.

---

* Maximus the Confessor, *"The Life of the Virgin"*, (Yale: Bloomsbury 2012), 96.

The Proclamation of the Kingdom and the Call to Conversion

THE FRUIT OF THIS MYSTERY

The fortitude to share the truths of the Catholic Faith with others

E ARMS THE TWELVE with miracles, saying, "Heal the sick, cleanse the lepers, raise the dead, cast out demons, freely you have received freely you should give." Nothing so befits a disciple as humility and non-possessiveness. Do not think so highly of yourselves, as if you had such good things to give from out of your own powers, no, you have received them as a gift and by grace. Furthermore, just as for that reason you must be humble, so also do not be lovers of money, for that reason, "freely give". (THEOPHYLACT)

OUR FATHER   Our Father, Who art in Heaven, hallowed be Thy name, Thy kingdom come, Thy will be done, on earth as it is in heaven. Give us this day our daily bread; and forgive us our trespasses, as we forgive those who trespass against us; and lead us not into temptation, but deliver us from evil. Amen.

HAIL MARY (10)   Hail Mary, Full of Grace, the Lord is with thee. Blessed art thou among women and blessed is the fruit of thy womb, Jesus. Holy Mary, Mother of God, pray for us sinners now, and at the hour of our death. Amen.

1. Before He spoke or did anything, Christ called Twelve Apostles, that neither His words nor deeds should be hid from their knowledge, so that afterwards they could say with confidence that they were preaching only the things they had seen. The operations of their secular craft were a prophecy of their future dignity. "Fishers of Men," that is, teachers, that with the net of God's word they might catch men out of this dangerous and stormy world, in which they are borne along by the Devil and by wicked pleasures. Yet these disciples did not follow Christ out of honour, the honour of being thought 'teachers', but rather because they prized the greatness of the labour itself; they saw how precious is the soul of a single man, they knew how much God desired man's salvation, and they marvelled at what great heavenly reward awaited those who

would leave all to share in Christ's labour. (FIFTH CENTURY, PSEUDO CHRYSOSTOM)

2. For by the net of holy preaching they drew fish, that is, men, from the depths of the sea, that is, out of infidelity, to the light of faith. Wonderful indeed is this fishing! For fish when they are caught, soon after die; when men are caught by the word of preaching, they rather are made alive. (REMIGANDUS)

3. Jesus said to Thomas, "Go to the lad who has the five barley loaves, and the two fish and bring him over to Me." Andrew replied, "Master, what will these five loaves be among so great a multitude as this?" Jesus said to him, "Bring them to Me, and the I will take care of this." And so he brought the lad to Jesus, and the boy said, "Master, I have toiled much for these." Jesus answered to him, "Give Me the five loaves which have been entrusted to you. Give them to Me for a wonderful work, and for an everlasting memorial, and for food that all may be filled." And Jesus took the loaves, and He gave thanks over them, and He broke them, and He gave them to the apostles to set them before the multitudes. (FIFTH CENTURY, SAHIDIC SERMON FRAGMENTS)

4. "From there the Lord Jesus went forth again to Nazareth with His holy mother, because Joseph, the one to whom the holy Virgin had initially been betrothed, had completed one hundred and ten years full of excellent days, he who had been worthy to be the parent and servant of the Lord and king of all and God, Jesus Christ. And he became an eyewitness to the ineffable wonders of His birth and upbringing and, after His baptism, to His miracles. Thus he went forth to eternal

life, and he received a blessing from the Lord Jesus Christ." **
(ST. MAXIMUS THE CONFESSOR)

5. King Abgar, who ruled with great glory the nations beyond
the Euphrates, being afflicted with a terrible disease which it
was beyond the power of human skill to cure, when he heard
of the name of Jesus, and of His miracles, which were attested
by all with one accord, sent a message to Him by a courier
and begged Him to heal his disease. But The Lord did not
at that time comply with his request; yet He deemed him
worthy of a personal letter in which He said that He would
send one of His disciples to cure his disease, and at the same
time promised salvation to himself and all his house. Not long
afterward His promise was fulfilled. For after His resurrection
from the dead and His ascent into heaven, Thomas, one of
the twelve apostles, under divine impulse sent Thaddeus to
Edessa, as a preacher and evangelist of the teaching of Christ.
And all that our Saviour had promised received through him
its fulfilment. (EUSEBIUS OF CAESAREA)

6. The Lord instructs them, "Be wise as serpents, and innocent
as doves." He wants the disciples to be wise, knowing how
to act when surrounded by many enemies. For just as the
serpent allows all the rest of its body to be struck but guards
its head, so let the Christian give all of his belongings and
even his body to those who would strike it, but let him guard
his head, which is Christ, and faith in Him. And just as the
serpent squeezes through a narrow hole and sheds its old

** Maximus the Confessor, *"The Life of the Virgin"*, (Yale: Bloomsbury
2012), 96.

skin, so too let us traverse the narrow way and shed the old man. But since a serpent is also poisonous, He commands us to be innocent, that is, sincere, guileless and harmless as doves. For even when a dove's offspring are taken from it and when it is driven away, it still flies back again to its masters. Be wise, then, as the serpent lest you be tricked in this life, but be blameless in all your ways, that is as guileless as the dove. (THEOPHYLACT)

7. The one that St. Luke calls a sinner, and that St. John names Mary, is the same woman from which the Lord has cast out seven demons. And what are these seven demons, if not the universality of all vices? Since seven days suffice to embrace the whole of time, the number seven rightly represents universality. Mary Magdalen had seven demons in her, for she was full of all vices. But now, having seen the stains that dishonoured her, she ran to wash herself at the source of mercy, without blushing in the presence of the guests. So great was her shame inside that she could not see anything outside to blush. When I think of Mary Magdalen's repentance, I feel more like crying than saying something. Indeed, what heart, even if it were of stone, would not be moved by the example of penance that the tears of this sinner give us? She considered what she had done, and did not want to limit what she was going to do. Here she enters among the guests, she comes uninvited, and, at the feast, she offers her tears most openly. Learn with what pain this woman is burning, she who does not blush to cry even in the middle of a banquet. (ST. GREGORY THE GREAT)

8. Mary Magdalen brought an alabaster vase full of perfume, and kneeling down before Jesus, she began to water His feet with her tears and to wipe them with the hair of her head; and

she kissed them, and sprinkled them with perfume. It is very evident, my brethren, that this woman, formerly addicted to forbidden deeds, had used perfume to give her flesh a pleasant odour. What she had shamefully granted to herself, she now offered to God in a manner worthy of praise. She had desired the things of the earth by her eyes, but now mortifying them with penance, she was crying. She had emphasised the beauty of her hair to adorn her face, but she was now using it to wipe away her tears. Her mouth had uttered words of pride, but now, kissing the feet of the Lord, she was pledging to walk in the humble footsteps of her Redeemer. Thus, she turned her crimes into so many virtues, and all that in her had despised God in sin was put to the service of God in penance. (ST. GREGORY THE GREAT)

9. Now there was a certain wealthy woman, Veronica by name, who dwelt in Paneas a city of Judaea. And having from childhood been afflicted with an issue of blood, she went to the physicians, expending all her wealth, yet found no cure. But hearing at last of the cures of the wonderful Christ, Who raised the dead, restored sight to the blind, cast out demons from mortals, and healed with a word all who pined away in sickness, she too ran to Him as to a god. Seeing the crowd surrounding Him, and fearing to tell Him of her incurable disease, she thought within herself that if she could but take hold of the hem of His garment, she should be altogether healed. So, secretly entering the multitude around her, she stole a cure by touching Christ's hem. The fountain of her blood stayed, and suddenly she became well. But He the more, as foreknowing the purpose of her heart, cried out, "Who touched Me? For power has gone out of Me." And she,

turning pale, and groaning, supposing the disease would return upon her more violently, falling before Him, flooded the ground with tears, confessing her daring. But He, being good, had compassion on her, and confirmed her cure, saying, "Daughter, take heart, your faith has delivered you; go in peace." (FOURTH CENTURY, 'THE STORY OF VERONICA')

10. The blind man knew of the Lord by His fame, and so he seized the opportunity when he heard that Jesus was passing by on the way. He believed that Jesus was able to heal him, and as his faith was exceedingly fervent, he did not fall silent when he was rebuked but cried out all the more. Therefore Jesus does not ask him if he has faith, but rather, what it is he wants. By His touch the Lord heals him, that we may learn that every member of His holy flesh was also a life-creating member of God. Understand that this blind man symbolises the Gentiles. Just as the blind man by hearing learned of Jesus, so too the Gentiles by hearing believed. Those who rebuked the blind man, telling him not to shout the name of Jesus, are the persecuting tyrants who attempted to shut the mouth of the Church, but she all the more confessed the name of Christ. Therefore She was healed and sees ever more clearly the light of the Truth, and follows Christ, imitating His life. (THEOPHYLACT)

GLORY BE TO THE FATHER   Glory be to the Father, and to the Son, and to the Holy Spirit, as it was in the beginning, is now and ever shall be, world without end. Amen.

THE FATIMA PRAYER   O my Jesus, forgive us our sins, save us from the fires of hell, lead all souls to heaven, especially those in most need of Thy mercy.

The Transfiguration of Our Lord on Mount Tabor

A desire to stay near to Lord through the intimacy of prayer, as a refuge in the storms of this passing world

PON MOUNT TABOR, JESUS revealed to His disciples a heavenly mystery. To banish from their hearts any possible doubt concerning the Kingdom and to confirm their faith in what lay in the future, He gave them on

Mount Tabor a wonderful vision of His glory, a foreshadowing
of the Kingdom of Heaven. It was as if He said to them, "As
time goes by you may be in danger of losing your faith. To
save you from this, I will allow you to see the Son of Man
coming in the glory of His Father." (ST. ATHANASIUS)

OUR FATHER   Our Father, Who art in Heaven, hallowed be
Thy name, Thy kingdom come, Thy will be done, on earth as
it is in heaven. Give us this day our daily bread; and forgive us
our trespasses, as we forgive those who trespass against us; and
lead us not into temptation, but deliver us from evil. Amen.

HAIL MARY (10)   Hail Mary, Full of Grace, the Lord is
with thee. Blessed art thou among women and blessed is the
fruit of thy womb, Jesus. Holy Mary, Mother of God, pray
for us sinners now, and at the hour of our death. Amen.

1. When the Lord was about to show His disciples the glory
of His brightness, He led them up the mountain, as it follows,
"And He took them up into a high mountain apart." Here the
Lord teaches that it is necessary for all who seek to contemplate God, not to grovel in weak and worldly pleasures, but,
by love of things above, to be ever raising themselves towards
heavenly things. (REMIGANDUS)

2. He took these three, Peter, James and John and in doing so
He set them before the others. But observe how the apostle
and evangelist Matthew does not conceal the names of these
three who had been preferred to himself; and in a like manner how John the Evangelist records the pre-eminent praise

given to Peter. See in this how the company of apostles was free from jealousy and vainglory. (ST. JOHN CHRYSOSTOM)

3. He leads them apart. This also shows how even in this life the saints are spiritually separated from the wicked through their devotion and their faith. In the future this separation will be complete and utter. Many are called, but few are chosen. (REMIGANDUS)

4. The disciples fell asleep while Christ continued for a long time in prayer, but then afterwards, on awaking, they became spectators of splendid and glorious things. Peter, thinking perhaps that the time of the Kingdom of God had now arrived, proposes to make three dwellings on the mountain, one for Christ, and the others for Moses and Elijah, "But he did not know what he was saying." It was not the time of the consummation of the world, nor for the saints to take possession of the glorious bodies promised to them. How could it have been right for Christ to have stayed forever on that mountain and to have abandoned His purpose of suffering on our behalf? No, He redeemed all men by undergoing death in the flesh, and by conquering death by His resurrection. Peter truly did not know what he was saying. (ST. CYRIL OF ALEXANDRIA)

5. Let us run with confidence and joy to enter into the cloud like Moses and Elijah, or like James and John. Let us be caught up like Peter to behold the divine vision and to be transfigured by that glorious transfiguration. Let us retire from the world, detach ourselves from the earth, rise above the body, cut ourselves off from creatures and turn to the Creator, to Whom Peter in ecstasy exclaimed, "Lord, it is good for us to

be here." It is indeed good to be here, as you have said, Peter.
It is good to be with Jesus and to remain here for ever. What
greater happiness or higher honour could we have than to
be with God, to be made like Him and to live in His light?
(ST. ATHANASIUS)

6. Likewise, since each of us possesses God in his heart and
is being transformed into His divine image, we also should
cry out with joy, "It is good for us to be here." With Christ
dwelling inside of us all things shine with divine radiance,
there should be nothing in our hearts but peace, serenity and
stillness, for God is present. Here, in our hearts, Christ has
taken up His abode together with the Father, saying as He
enters, "Today salvation has come to this house." With Christ,
our hearts receive all the wealth of His eternal blessings, and
there we see reflected as in a mirror the whole of the world
to come. (ST. ATHANASIUS)

7. As the effulgence of the Son's body displayed the Son to
their sight, so the Father's voice from the cloud announced the
Father to their hearing. And when this voice was heard, the
disciples fell upon their faces and were very afraid, trembling
at the majesty, not only of the Father, but also of the Son:
for now the disciples had a deeper insight into the undivided
Deity of Both, and they knew not to separate the One from
the Other. (ST. LEO THE GREAT)

8. Three things cause the disciples to be frightened. Firstly,
they knew that they were sinners, secondly, because the bright
cloud had covered them, and finally, because they heard the
voice of God the Father speaking. Indeed, human frailty

cannot endure to look upon so great glory, and falls to the earth trembling, both in soul and in body. (ST. JEROME)

9. And although they had their faces to the floor, and could not raise themselves again, He approaches them and touches them gently, that by His touch their fear might be banished, and their unnerved limbs gain strength, "And Jesus drew near and touched them." But He further added His word to His hand, saying, "Arise, fear not." He banishes their fear, that He may after impart teaching. And they see Jesus standing alone, that the cloud has been removed, and that Moses and Elijah have disappeared. The shadow of the Law and Prophets have departed, for both are found in the Gospel. (ST. JEROME)

10. You were transfigured on the mountain, O Christ our God, Your disciples beheld Your glory as far as they could see it, so that when they would behold You crucified, they would understand that Your suffering was voluntary, and would proclaim to the world that You are truly the Radiance of the Father! Let Your everlasting Light also shine upon us sinners, through the prayers of the Mother of God. O Giver of Light, all glory to You! (NINTH CENTURY, BYZANTINE LITURGY)

GLORY BE TO THE FATHER   Glory be to the Father, and to the Son, and to the Holy Spirit, as it was in the beginning, is now and ever shall be, world without end. Amen.

THE FATIMA PRAYER   O my Jesus, forgive us our sins, save us from the fires of hell, lead all souls to heaven, especially those in most need of Thy mercy.

The Institution of the Holy Eucharist

THE FRUIT OF THIS MYSTERY

*A profound love for the sublime mystery of the real presence
of Our Lord Jesus in the Blessed Sacrament*

UR LORD JESUS TOOK in His hands what in the beginning was only bread, and He blessed it, and signed it, and made it holy in the name of the Father and in the name of the Spirit; and He broke it and in His gracious kindness He distributed it to all His disciples one by one. He said, "Take this, all of you, and eat of It, that

Which My word has made Holy. Do not regard what I am giving you as mere bread, It is the Bread of Life. Do not let any crumbs of It scatter, for I have called it My Body, and that It truly is." (ST. EPHREM)

OUR FATHER   Our Father, Who art in Heaven, hallowed be Thy name, Thy kingdom come, Thy will be done, on earth as it is in heaven. Give us this day our daily bread; and forgive us our trespasses, as we forgive those who trespass against us; and lead us not into temptation, but deliver us from evil. Amen.

HAIL MARY (10)   Hail Mary, Full of Grace, the Lord is with thee. Blessed art thou among women and blessed is the fruit of thy womb, Jesus. Holy Mary, Mother of God, pray for us sinners now, and at the hour of our death. Amen.

1. He sent Peter and John to the city, saying, "Follow the man carrying the pitcher of water and say to the master of the house, 'The Teacher says to you, where is the guest-chamber, where I may eat the passover with My disciples?'" The reason He did not plainly mention loudly all the details was because Judas had promised the Jews that he would deliver Christ to them, and was watching for an opportunity to hand Him over. Christ gives a sign to prevent Judas from learning in advance where the passover was to take place. When then the disciples had prepared the passover, Christ ate it with them, being long suffering towards the traitor, and deigning to admit him to the table from His infinite loving kindness. And Christ said to His holy apostles, "I have desired with a desire to eat this passover with you", meaning, "I have used all diligence to enable me to escape the wickedness of the

traitor, that I might not endure My passion before the time and before this meal." (ST. CYRIL OF ALEXANDRIA)

2. "And having risen from supper, He laid aside His garments." He does not merely wash the apostles' feet, but does so, putting off His garments. And He doesn't even stop here, but He girds Himself with a towel. And furthermore, not satisfied with this, He fills the basin Himself, not bidding another to fill it for Him. He did all these things Himself, giving us an example. Let us then, when we are engaged in doing good deeds, do so not merely for appearances sake, but with all zeal. (ST. JOHN CHRYSOSTOM)

3. Indeed, the Lord seems to me to have washed the feet of the traitor first. And Judas, though continually guilty, felt nothing. Jesus washed the man who had already chosen to betray Him. Even up to the last day, the Master continued to bear with him. He seems to me to have washed the traitor first, then to have come to Peter, and whilst Judas felt no compunction, Peter was so abashed, that being even distressed and trembling, He asked, "Lord, are You going to wash my feet?" (ST. JOHN CHRYSOSTOM)

4. When the Lord is about to break the bread He gives thanks, teaching us also to offer the Bread with thanksgiving. At the same time He also shows by this that He gladly accepts as a gift the breaking of His own Body, that is, His death, and that He is not displeased as if it were something that He is unwilling to accept. In like manner, we too might gladly accept martyrdom as a gift. By saying, "This is My Body", He shows that the bread which is sanctified on the altar is the

Lord's Body Itself, and not a symbolic type. For He did not say, "This is a type", but "This is My Body". By an ineffable action it is changed, although It may appear to us as bread. Since we are weak and could not endure to eat raw meat, much less human flesh, It appears as bread to us although It is indeed flesh. (THEOPHYLACT)

5. Jesus added, "One particle from its crumbs is able to sanctify thousands and thousands, and is sufficient to afford life to those who eat of It. Take, eat, entertaining no doubt of faith, because this is My Body, and whoever eats It in belief eats in It Fire and Spirit. But if any doubter eats of It, for him It will be only bread. And if anyone despises It or rejects It or treats It with dishonour, It may be taken as a certainty that He treats Me with dishonour, because I have called It and actually made It to be My Body." (ST. EPHREM)

6. In case we would be terrified by seeing blood filled flesh placed upon the holy tables of our churches, God, humbling Himself to our infirmities, infuses into the things set before us the power of life, and transforms them into His flesh. And so these mysteries are a life-giving participation in the body of Him, Who is the Life; a life-producing seed. Receive in faith the Saviour's word, for He, being the Truth, cannot lie. The words of God are of course true, and in no manner whatsoever can they be false, even if we cannot understand exactly the way in which God works and acts in cases such as this. How indeed can a man grasp such things which transcend the powers of our mind and reason? Let this, the divine mystery, be honoured by faith. (ST. CYRIL OF ALEXANDRIA)

7. When you cast a piece of bread into wine or oil, or any other liquid, you find that it becomes charged with the quality of that particular thing. When iron is brought into contact with fire, it becomes full of its activity; and while it is by nature iron, it exerts the power of fire. And so the life-giving Word of God endowed His flesh with the power of giving life. And of this He certifies us Himself, saying, "I am the living bread, that came down from heaven; if a man eat of this bread, he shall live for ever, and the bread that I shall give is My flesh for the life of the world." When therefore we eat the holy flesh of Christ, the Saviour of us all, and drink His precious blood, we have life in us, being made as it were, one with Him, and abiding in Him, and possessing Him also in us. (ST. CYRIL OF ALEXANDRIA)

8. When we speak of the reality of Christ's nature being inside of us, we would be speaking foolishly and impiously had we not learned it from Him. For He Himself says, "My flesh is truly food, and My blood is truly drink. He that eats My flesh and drinks My blood will remain in Me and I in Him." As to the reality of His flesh and blood, there is no room left for doubt, because now, both by the declaration of the Lord Himself and by our own faith, It is truly flesh and It is truly blood. And so when these elements are taken and consumed we are in Christ and Christ is in us. Is this not true? Let those who deny that Jesus Christ is true God be free to find these things untrue. But He Himself is in us through the flesh, and we are in Him. And because we are with Him, truly we are with God and in God, according to His divinity. (ST. HILARY OF POITIERS)

9. Notice the cruelty of Judas, worse than a beast, Judas fails to become more meek as he is invited to partake of this liturgical meal. Not even when reproved does he listen, but he even went so far as to taste of the Lord's Body, and still he did not repent. Perhaps however Christ did not give the Mysteries to Judas, it could have been that the other disciples only received Them after Judas had left. This would conform with the teaching we have received, that the Mysteries should be withheld from those who are evil. (THEOPHYLACT)

10. When you see the Lord sacrificed, and laid upon the altar, and the priest standing and praying over the victim, and all the worshippers filled with the precious blood, can you then think that you are still among men, and standing upon the earth? Are you not, on the contrary, translated to Heaven, and casting out every carnal thought from the soul, do you not contemplate the things which are in Heaven? Oh! What a marvel! What love of God to man! He who sits on high with the Father is at that hour held in the hands of priests, and gives Himself to those who are willing to embrace Him. All this can only be appreciated through the eyes of faith! (ST. JOHN CHRYSOSTOM)

GLORY BE TO THE FATHER   Glory be to the Father, and to the Son, and to the Holy Spirit, as it was in the beginning, is now and ever shall be, world without end. Amen.

THE FATIMA PRAYER   O my Jesus, forgive us our sins, save us from the fires of hell, lead all souls to heaven, especially those in most need of Thy mercy.

CONCLUDING PRAYERS   *Upon completing the recitation of the Holy Rosary, the following prayers are customary, but others too may be added according to one's devotion and preference.*

HAIL HOLY QUEEN PRAYER   Hail Holy Queen, Mother of Mercy, hail our life, our sweetness and our hope. To thee do we cry, poor banished children of Eve, to thee do we send up our sighs, mourning and weeping in this vale of tears. Turn then, most gracious advocate, thine eyes of mercy towards us, and after this, our exile, show unto us the blessed fruit of thy womb, Jesus. O clement, O loving, O sweet Virgin Mary. Pray for us O holy Mother of God, that we may be made worthy of the promises of Christ.

Let Us Pray   O God, Whose only begotten son, by His life, death and resurrection, has purchased for us the rewards of eternal life, grant we beseech Thee, that meditating on these mysteries of the most Holy Rosary of the Blessed Virgin Mary, we may both imitate what they contain and obtain what they promise, through the same Christ our Lord. Amen.

SAINT MICHAEL THE ARCHANGEL PRAYER   Holy Michael, the Archangel, defend us in the day of battle. Be our safeguard against the wickedness and snares of the devil. May God rebuke him, we humbly pray; and do thou, O Prince of the heavenly hosts, by the power of God thrust down into hell Satan and all the evil spirits who wander through the world seeking the ruin of souls. Amen.

MEMORARE PRAYER   Remember, O most gracious Virgin Mary, that never was it known that anyone who fled to thy protection, implored thy help, or sought thine intercession was left unaided. Inspired by this confidence, I fly unto thee, O Virgin of virgins, my mother; to thee do I come, before thee I stand, sinful and sorrowful. O Mother of the Word Incarnate, despise not my petitions, but in thy mercy hear and answer me. Amen.

May the Divine Assistance remain always with us, and may the souls of the faithful departed, through the mercy of God rest in peace. Amen.

The Hopeful Mysteries

The Creation of all Things in Christ

THE FRUIT OF THIS MYSTERY

Adoration of the power and wisdom of Almighty God

CHRIST WAS LIKE A blameless and spotless lamb, foreordained from the foundation of the world. Christ is the blessed end on account of which everything was created. This is the divine purpose, which was thought of before the beginning of Creation, and which we call the intended fulfilment. This is the mystery circumscribing all ages, the awesome plan of God. For on account of Christ, that is to say the mystery concerning Christ, all time, and all that which is in time, have found the beginning and end of their existence. (ST. MAXIMUS THE CONFESSOR)

OUR FATHER   Our Father, Who art in Heaven, hallowed be Thy name, Thy kingdom come, Thy will be done, on earth as it is in heaven. Give us this day our daily bread; and forgive us our trespasses, as we forgive those who trespass against us; and lead us not into temptation, but deliver us from evil. Amen.

HAIL MARY (10)   Hail Mary, Full of Grace, the Lord is with thee. Blessed art thou among women and blessed is the fruit of thy womb, Jesus. Holy Mary, Mother of God, pray for us sinners now, and at the hour of our death. Amen.

1. "In the beginning God created the heavens and the earth." In the same way that the potter does not exhaust either his art or his talent in creating many pots of clay; so worked the Maker of the universe, Whose creative power is infinite. The Creator needed only the impulse of His will to bring the immensities of the visible world into being. And Who is this Creator? Let His name be engraved into our hearts, it is God. In the beginning God created, It is He, the Benevolent One, goodness without measure, the worthy object of our love, the beauty most to be desired, the origin of all that exists, the source of life and of impenetrable wisdom, it is He Who in the beginning created the heavens and the earth. (ST. BASIL OF CAESAREA)

2. Before land existed, before the mountains were settled, before the fountains burst forth, the Son took upon Himself

the plan to save us. And so even though the earth, and the mountains, and the shapes of visible nature will all pass away, we, on the contrary, shall not grow old after their pattern. We may be able to live after they have all passed, having the spiritual life and blessing which, before these things were created, was prepared for us in the Christ. (ST. ATHANASIUS)

3. But consider how great and admirable is the holy prophet Moses. The other prophets predicted events which were to be realised in a very distant time. This one however, who lived centuries after the creation of the world, was inspired to tell us the ancient work of the Lord. "In the beginning God created the heavens and the earth." God alone Who worked these wonders leads and directs the tongue of the prophet to teach us. Let all human reasoning here be silenced. Do not to listen to this narrative as if it were merely the word of Moses. It is God himself Who speaks to us, and Moses is only His interpreter. The reasoning of man, says scripture, is timid, and his thoughts uncertain. Let us, then, accept the divine word with humble deference, without exceeding the limits of our intelligence, nor curiously seeking what it cannot attain. To deny that a creator God has drawn all thing from nothing would be the height of madness. "In the beginning God created the heavens and the earth." (ST. JOHN CHRYSOSTOM)

4. "And God said, 'Let there be light'." The first word of God created the nature of light, it made darkness vanish, dispelled gloom, illuminated the world, and gave to all beings at the same time a sweet and gracious aspect. The heavens, until then enveloped in darkness, appeared with that beauty which they still present to our eyes. The sky was lit up and the

splendour spread rapidly in every direction, dispersing itself
to the extreme limits of the heavens. In an instant it lighted
up the whole extent of the world, the North and the South,
the East and the West. With a single word and in one instant,
the Creator of all things gives the gift of light to our world.
The utterance of the Divine Word gives light to every object
and radiates them with beauty. (ST. BASIL OF CAESAREA)

5. God fashioned man out of the visible and invisible creation
into His own image and likeness to reign as king and ruler
over the earth and all creation. But first He made for him
a kingdom in which he should live a life of happiness and
prosperity. And this is the divine paradise, planted in Eden,
by the hands of God, a very storehouse of joy and gladness of
heart, indeed "Eden" means 'luxuriousness'. Its site is higher
in the East than all the earth, it is temperate and the air that
surrounds it is the rarest and purest, evergreen plants are its
pride, sweet fragrances abound, it is flooded with light, and
in sensuous freshness and beauty it transcends imagination.
In truth the place is divine, it is a fitting home for him who
was created in God's image. (ST. JOHN DAMASCENE)

6. God says, "Let us make man in Our own image, and after
Our own likeness", He speaks as a Trinity of persons. The
Father had His Son close at His side, His own Word, and
the third Person too, the Holy Spirit. God made man in the
likeness of The Son, Who was one day to put on human nature,
and the Spirit, Who was to sanctify man. (TERTULLIAN)

7. It is certain that, from the very beginning of his nature, man
was endowed with the instinct to sleep. Adam slept before he

laboured, before he ate, in fact, even before he spoke. And indeed, we are led to trace the image of death in Adam's first slumber. For just as Adam was a figure of Christ, Adam's sleep foreshadowed the death of Christ, Who was to sleep a mortal slumber on the cross. Contemplate the wound inflicted on the side of Christ while He slept in death, and see how just as Eve was formed while Adam slept, so the church, the true mother of the living, came forth from Christ. For this reason even our sleep is so salutary, so rational. God wills to set before us many teachings through types and shadows. (TERTULLIAN)

8. The tree of life which was planted by God in Paradise pre-figured the precious Cross of Christ. For since death was by a tree, it was fitting that life and resurrection should be bestowed by a tree. In the cross is the perfection of those that press forwards, the salvation of soul and body, the taking away of sin. Here is the plant of the resurrection, the tree of eternal life. (ST. JOHN DAMASCENE)

9. God gave Adam a commandment as befitting a creature of free will, He told Adam which plants that he might partake of and which one he might not touch. This latter was the tree of knowledge; not, however, because it was evil from the beginning when planted, nor was it forbidden because God was threatened by our eating of it, as the wicked serpent had suggested. No, surely it would have been good for man but only when partaken of at the proper time. The tree would have bestowed the gift of 'contemplation', something safe and good only for those who have reached a maturity of habit to enter upon it, a 'solid food', good for those who

are no longer tender and only capable of receiving milk. (ST. GREGORY THE THEOLOGIAN)

10. Consider, I invite you, the eminent happiness of our first parents. How high they were above all sensible and gross creatures! They dwelt less on the earth than the sky; and although clothed with a body, they did not feel infirmities, and so they did not need a roof, nor clothes, nor any other external help. Their life was exempt from sorrow and sadness, their condition was almost that of angels. Neither man nor woman feared any animal, for each creature recognised their empire and authority. Wild and ferocious beasts were as submissive as pets are today. Adam and Eve were naked and they did not blush. But indeed, how could they have known their nakedness, for the heavenly glory itself would have been as a splendid garment. (ST JOHN CHRYSOSTOM)

GLORY BE TO THE FATHER   Glory be to the Father, and to the Son, and to the Holy Spirit, as it was in the beginning, is now and ever shall be, world without end. Amen.

THE FATIMA PRAYER   O my Jesus, forgive us our sins, save us from the fires of hell, lead all souls to heaven, especially those in most need of Thy mercy.

The Promise of the Redeemer and Co-Redemptrix

THE FRUIT OF THE MYSTERY

Gratitude to Almighty God for the plan of salvation

"I WILL PUT ENMITY BETWEEN you and the woman; between your posterity and hers." It is as if God says: "It is not enough to see you crawling on the earth, I will make woman your irreconcilable enemy, so that war will always subsist between your posterity and hers. At last she will crush your head, and you will insidiously wound her in the heel. Yes, I will give her seed the strength to walk on your head, and you will shake in vain under His feet." This punishment of the serpent shows to us the great goodness of the Lord with regard to man. What scripture says here about the serpent above all applies to the devil. And indeed, to humble this proud spirit, God compels him to crawl under our feet, and, through Christ, He gives us too the power to crush his head. (ST. JOHN CHRYSOSTOM)

OUR FATHER   Our Father, Who art in Heaven, hallowed be Thy name, Thy kingdom come, Thy will be done, on earth as it is in heaven. Give us this day our daily bread; and forgive us our trespasses, as we forgive those who trespass against us; and lead us not into temptation, but deliver us from evil. Amen.

HAIL MARY (10)   Hail Mary, Full of Grace, the Lord is with thee. Blessed art thou among women and blessed is the fruit of thy womb, Jesus. Holy Mary, Mother of God, pray for us sinners now, and at the hour of our death. Amen.

1. Notice how the angel's sin is concealed in silence in Genesis while man's is revealed, this is because God did not predestine that the angel's wound would be cured, whereas for man's He had predestined a cure. Indeed, the sin of the highest angel could not be cured, for the angel was the inventor of his own crime, whereas man was seduced by the devil's deceit. Furthermore, inasmuch as the angel was higher in glory, so much greater was his fall, whereas as much as man is weaker in nature, so much easier is it for him to obtain forgiveness. Man, made free in God's image, must prove himself worthy of

praise through choosing to do good, or worthy of damnation through desiring evil. (ST. ALCUIN OF YORK)

2. "The serpent was more subtle than any of the beasts of the earth", not on account of his own nature, but because of the inspiration of the diabolical spirit. For the Devil was using the serpent as an instrument to perpetrate the malice of his cunning. Just as a demoniac or madman speaks things that he does not know, so the serpent uttered words beyond its understanding. Eve listen and believed the words of this serpent, perhaps because there already was in her mind a certain love of her own power and a certain presumption concerning herself, a quality that was needing to be freely overcome and subdued. (ST. ALCUIN OF YORK)

3. For our ancient enemy ceases not daily to do the very same thing which he did in Paradise. For he endeavours to pluck out the words of God from the hearts of men, and to plant therein the false blandishments of his own promising. He, day by day, softens down the threatenings of God and invites us to believe in his own false words. For he falsely promises temporal blessings in order to soften down in men's minds the eternal punishments which God threatens. (ST. GREGORY OF ROME)

4. "So they ate it and their eyes opened", but to what? Alas, to the fires of concupiscence, the pain of sin, which, with death, had been insinuated into their flesh. This was no longer just that animal body which might be transformed into a more perfect and spiritual body without passing through death, no, now it became a flesh of death and a law now fought

within it against the law of the spirit. In this confusion they had recourse to fig leaves, they made themselves belts, and, for renouncing a glorious state, concealed their shameful nakedness. (ST. AUGUSTINE)

5. "They heard the voice of the Lord, Who was coming into the garden about the middle of the day." The Lord wanted to make them feel their fault by bringing them to extreme anguish of mind and heart. This is what happened, they were so ashamed that at the approach of God they hid themselves, and indeed, this incorruptible judge, whom we call conscience, rose up against them and accused them aloud. Conscience does this to us all, she puts our sins before our eyes, and represents to us all their stupidity. God, in creating man, establishes within himself that censor that never stops and that can not be deceived. In whatever place the guilty man transports himself, he carries within himself that conscience which accuses him, disturbs him, tears him up, and never rests. She attacks him in the intimacy of the man's own home, in the street and in meetings. She pursues him during feasts, during his sleep and when he wakes up. She never ceases to ask him to account for his faults and to bring before his eyes the gravity and the punishment. Conscience is then a charitable physician who assiduously accompanies the patient, and, in spite of his rejections, persists in offering him a remedy. (ST. JOHN CHRYSOSTOM)

6. And then, at that moment, the mother of Our Lord Jesus Christ was already promised. It is she who was made the opponent of the serpent's enmities. God says, "I will put enmities between you and the woman." He does not say,

"I put," lest it might seem to refer to Eve, but "I will put," relating to Mary. And God foretells of the achievement of this Virgin, namely, she shall trample on the serpent's head. (FIFTH CENTURY, PSEUDO JEROME)

7. Thus was announced the ancient hatred, the fierce enmity between the asp and man. And now the serpent is prostrate, he is crushed under the woman's feet. For having merited to bring forth God, the Virgin makes all his poisons powerless. (AURELIUS PRUDENTIUS)

8. Truly Lord ,You and Your Mother are the only ones who are absolutely and completely beautiful, for there is no guilt in You, Lord, nor any stain your Mother. Adam did not engender You, nor did his son who unjustly killed his brother. You are the children of the Holy Spirit. The Devil came, raging very much, and puffed with pride. Mary's Son trampled on him sorely, yet he is a serpent who, though crushed, still attacks. (ST. EPHREM)

9. The Lord said that He saw Satan fall from heaven. That accursed one had exalted himself but he was cast down from his high place. The foot of Mary trampled on him who had struck at Eve on her heel. Blessed is He, Our Lord Jesus Christ, who laid the devil low by His holy birth. (ST. EPHREM)

10. What then is the enemy of the human race likely to say to himself when now he sees us adopted as sons through the working of this woman? Does he not ask repeatedly and lament, "How has it happened that the instrument who was my colleague in the beginning is now my enemy? A woman

co-operated with me to obtain power over their race, and now woman has dethroned me. The ancient Eve exalted me, but the New Eve deposed me. Rightly then have I been taken captive by her whom I conquered, for she gave birth to the One Who despoiled me from the cross, and caused the dead to rise together with Him. Now who was the cause of all this but she who gave birth to Him? It would have been better for me never to have led the ancient Eve into deceiving Adam; it would have been better for me never to have taken possession of that serpent" (CHRYSIPPUS OF CAPPADOCIA)

GLORY BE TO THE FATHER   Glory be to the Father, and to the Son, and to the Holy Spirit, as it was in the beginning, is now and ever shall be, world without end. Amen.

THE FATIMA PRAYER   O my Jesus, forgive us our sins, save us from the fires of hell, lead all souls to heaven, especially those in most need of Thy mercy.

The Birth of the Immaculate Virgin

FRUIT OF THE MYSTERY

A Devotion to the Holy Infancy of the Blessed Virgin

ANN WAS TO BE the mother of the Virgin Mother of God, and hence nature did not dare to anticipate the flowering of grace. Thus nature remained sterile until grace produced its fruit. Mary was to be born a first born daughter since she would be the mother of the First-Born of all Creation, in Whom all things are held together. And so rejoice, Ann, that you were sterile and have not borne children; break forth into shouts, you who have not given birth. Rejoice, Joachim, because from your daughter a child is born for us, a son is given us, Whose name is Messenger of Great Counsel and Mighty God. (ST. JOHN DAMASCENE)

OUR FATHER   Our Father, Who art in Heaven, hallowed be Thy name, Thy kingdom come, Thy will be done, on earth as it is in heaven. Give us this day our daily bread; and forgive us our trespasses, as we forgive those who trespass against us; and lead us not into temptation, but deliver us from evil. Amen.

HAIL MARY (10)   Hail Mary, Full of Grace, the Lord is with thee. Blessed art thou among women and blessed is the fruit of thy womb, Jesus. Holy Mary, Mother of God, pray for us sinners now, and at the hour of our death. Amen.

1. In those days there was a man in Jerusalem, Joachim by name, of the tribe of Judah. He was the shepherd of his own sheep, fearing the Lord in integrity and singleness of heart. He had no other care than that of his herds, from the produce of which he supplied with food all who feared God. And as he did so the Lord multiplied his herds, so that there was no man like him in the people of Israel. At the age of twenty he took Ann for his wife, the daughter of Achar, of his own tribe, the tribe of Judah, of the family of David. And though they had lived together for twenty years, he had by her neither sons nor daughters. And it happened that, in the time of the feast, among those who were offering incense to the Lord, Joachim stood getting ready his gifts in the sight of the Lord. And the priest, Ruben by name, coming to him, said, "It is not lawful for you to stand among those who are

doing sacrifice to God, because God has not blessed you so as to give you seed in Israel." Being therefore put to shame in the sight of the people, he retired in tears from the temple of the Lord and did not return to his house. (FOURTH CENTURY, PSEUDO MATTHEW)

2. Ann was God-loving, wise, but unable to conceive; she lived in harmony with her husband, but they were childless. And whilst she kept the observance of the law of the Lord, she was daily stung by the grief of childlessness with sorrow and distress. And whilst Joachim and his spouse lamented that they had no successor to continue their line, the spark of hope was not extinguished in them completely: both intensified their prayer about the granting to them of a child. In imitation of the prayer of Hannah, both came frequently to the temple and fervently beseeched God that He would undo Ann's sterility and make fruitful her childlessness. And they did not give up on their efforts until their wish was fulfilled. (ST. ANDREW OF CRETE)

3. At that time, a young man appeared to Joachim on the mountains while he was feeding his flocks, and said to him, "Why don't you return to your wife?" And Joachim said, "I have been with her for twenty years, and it has not been the will of God to give me children by her. I have been driven with shame and reproach from the temple of the Lord, why should I go back to her, when I have been so utterly despised? Here then will I remain with my sheep; and so long as in this life God is willing to grant me light, I shall willingly, by the hands of my servants, bestow their portions upon the poor, and the orphans, and those that fear God." And when he

had finished speaking, the young man said to him, "I am an angel of the Lord, and I have today appeared to your wife when she was weeping and praying, and have consoled her; and know that she has conceived a daughter from your seed, and you, in your ignorance of this, have left her. The child will dwell in the temple of God, and the Holy Spirit shall abide in her; and her blessedness shall be greater than that of all the holy women, so that no one can say that any before her has been like her, or that any after her in this world will be so. Therefore go down from the mountains and return to your wife, whom you will find to be pregnant. For God has raised up seed in her, and for this you will give God thanks; and her seed shall be blessed, and she herself shall be blessed, and shall be made the mother of eternal blessing." (FOURTH CENTURY, PSEUDO MATTHEW)

4. And when, after thirty days, Joachim was nearby once again, behold, the angel of the Lord appeared to Ann, who was standing and praying, and said, "Go to the gate which is called Golden, and meet your husband there, for today he will come to you." She therefore went towards him in haste with her maidens, and, praying to the Lord, she stood a long time in the gate waiting for him. And when she was wearied with long waiting, she lifted up her eyes and saw Joachim afar off coming with his flocks; and she ran to him and hung on his neck, giving thanks to God, and saying: "I was a widow, and behold now I am not so: I was barren, and behold I have now conceived." And so they worshipped the Lord and went into their own house. And when this was heard of, there was great joy among all their neighbours and acquaintances, so

that the whole land of Israel congratulated them. (FOURTH CENTURY, PSEUDO MATTHEW)

5. And when her months were fulfilled, in the ninth month, Ann brought forth. And she said to the midwife, "What have I brought forth?" And she said, "A girl," and Ann replied, "My soul has been magnified this day", and she laid her down. And the days having been fulfilled, Ann was purified, and fed the child with her milk, and the child was named Mary. (SECOND CENTURY, THE PROTOEVANGELIUM OF JAMES)

6. God, the bestower of gifts, did not scorn the gift of hope that He had given to them. His unceasing power came quickly in help to that holy couple who prayed and beseeched Him. And so He made capable both the one and the other to produce and bear a child. In such manner, from sterile and barren parents, as it were from irrigated trees, was borne for us a most glorious fruition, the all-pure Virgin. The constraints of infertility were destroyed, prayer, upright manner of life, these rendered them fruitful. The childless begat a child, and the childless woman was made a happy mother. Thus the immaculate fruition issuing forth from the womb occurred from an infertile mother, and then the parents promised her to God and to His service in the temple. (ST. ANDREW OF CRETE)

7. Through your holy birth, O Immaculate One, Joachim and Ann were freed from the reproach of childlessness, and Adam and Eve from the corruption of death. Delivered from the guilt of sin, your people celebrate and cry out to you. The one who is barren gives birth to the Mother of God, the sustainer of our life. (ST. ROMANOS THE MELODIST)

8. The present festival, the birth of the Mother of God, is the prelude, while the final act is the fore-ordained union of the Word with flesh. Today the Virgin is born, tended, formed and prepared for her role as Mother of God, the universal king of the ages. Darkness yields before the coming of the light. Let all creation sing and dance and unite to make worthy contribution to the celebration of this day. Let there be one common festival for saints in heaven and men on earth. Let everything, mundane things and those above, join in festive celebration. Today this created world is raised to the dignity of a holy place for Him Who made all things. The creature is newly prepared to be a divine dwelling place for the Creator. (ST. ANDREW OF CRETE)

9. Joachim and Ann, how chaste a couple! While safeguarding the chastity prescribed by the law of nature, you achieved with God's help something which transcends nature in giving the world the Virgin Mother of God as your daughter. While leading a devout and holy life in your human nature, you gave birth to a daughter nobler than the angels, whose queen she now is. Girl of utter beauty and delight, daughter of Adam and mother of God, blessed the loins and blessed the womb from which you come! Blessed are the arms that carried you, and blessed are your parents' lips, which you covered with chaste kisses. Rejoice in God, all the earth, exult and sing hymns, raise your voice, raise it and have no fear. (ST. JOHN DAMASCENE)

10. Today the Son of the Carpenter, the Word Who fashioned all things, has prepared for himself a living ladder whose base has been set on earth and whose top reaches to heaven itself.

Today the gate that looks eastward, through which Christ will come in and go out, has been built. Inside it is Christ, and through Him we have gained access to the Father. Indeed, for blessed Ann, an oyster is born, the one who will conceive in her womb. Within this oyster the heavenly lightning-flash of divinity will strike, and in her will bear the pearl of great price, Our Lord Jesus Christ. (ST. JOHN DAMASCENE)

GLORY BE TO THE FATHER   Glory be to the Father, and to the Son, and to the Holy Spirit, as it was in the beginning, is now and ever shall be, world without end. Amen.

THE FATIMA PRAYER   O my Jesus, forgive us our sins, save us from the fires of hell, lead all souls to heaven, especially those in most need of Thy mercy.

The Presentation of Mary, as a Girl, in the Temple

FRUIT OF THE MYSTERY

A desire to remain in God's presence, before the tabernacle

MARY FIRST SAW THE light of day in the house of Joachim and Ann near the pool of Bethesda, and later, she was brought to the temple. Like a flower planted in the house of God, nurtured by the Holy Spirit, like a fruitful olive tree, she became the abode of all virtues.

She dispelled from her mind every desire of this life or of the flesh. She preserved virginity in soul and body, as was befitting the one was to receive God into her womb. (ST. JOHN DAMASCENE)

OUR FATHER   Our Father, Who art in Heaven, hallowed be Thy name, Thy kingdom come, Thy will be done, on earth as it is in heaven. Give us this day our daily bread; and forgive us our trespasses, as we forgive those who trespass against us; and lead us not into temptation, but deliver us from evil. Amen.

HAIL MARY (10)   Hail Mary, Full of Grace, the Lord is with thee. Blessed art thou among women and blessed is the fruit of thy womb, Jesus. Holy Mary, Mother of God, pray for us sinners now, and at the hour of our death. Amen.

1. And the child was two years old, and Joachim said, "Let us take her up to the temple of the Lord, that we may pay the vow that we have made." And Ann said, "Let us wait for the third year, in order that the child may not seek for its father or mother." And Joachim said, "So let us wait." And the child was three years old, and Joachim said, "Invite the daughters of the Hebrews that are undefiled, and let them each take a lamp, and let them stand with the lamps burning, that the child might not turn back, and that her heart might be captivated with the temple of the Lord." The priest received Mary, and kissed her, and blessed her, saying, "The Lord has magnified your name in all generations. In you, on the last of the days, the Lord will manifest His redemption to the sons of Israel." And Joachim set her down upon the third step of the temple, and the Lord God sent grace upon her; and she skipped

joyfully as she went up, and all the house of Israel loved her. (SECOND CENTURY, THE PROTOEVANGELIUM OF JAMES)

2. In fulfilment of her vow, today, Ann, with joy, brings to the temple of the Lord the true temple and pure Mother of God. Today the universe is filled with joy at the glorious feast of the Mother of God, and cries out, "She is the heavenly tabernacle." (NINTH CENTURY, BYZANTINE LITURGY)

3. The parents of the Immaculate, in the first blossoming of her growth brought her to the temple and dedicated her to God. The priest who was leading the ceremony beheld the face of the girl and became gladdened and joyful, seeing the actual fulfilment of the divine promise. He consecrated her to God, as a gift and sacrifice. Then he led this great treasury of salvation into the very innermost parts of the temple. Here the maiden walked in the upright ways of the Lord, as in bridal chambers, partaking of heavenly food until the time of betrothal, which was preordained before all the ages. (ST. ANDREW OF CRETE)

4. In her third year, Joachim and Ann went together to the temple of the Lord to offer sacrifices to God, and they placed the infant, Mary by name, in the community of virgins, who remained day and night praising God. And when she was put down before the doors of the temple, she went up the fifteen steps so swiftly, that she did not look back at all, nor, like other young children, did she continue to long for her parents. (FOURTH CENTURY, PSEUDO MATTHEW)

5. Ann, the all-praised, cried out rejoicing, "Receive O Zechariah, her whom God's prophets proclaimed in the Spirit. Bring her into the holy Temple, there to be brought up in reverence, that she may become the divine throne of the Master of all, that she may become His palace and resting place, a dwelling filled with light!" (NINTH CENTURY, BYZANTINE LITURGY)

6. At that time, the High Priest was in ecstasy, filled with the Spirit of God, and understood that the maiden was the dwelling place of divine grace and more worthy then he to stand always before God's countenance. He remembered that the law commended the ark be placed in the Holy of Holies and straight away perceived that this ordinance pertained to the maiden." (THEOPHYLACT)

7. Go, O Queen of the world, O Mother of God, go joyfully to the house of God, there to await the coming of the Divine Spirit, Who will make you the Mother of the Eternal Word. Enter with exultation the courts of the Lord, in expectation of the coming of the Holy Ghost, and the Conception of the only-begotten Son of God (ST. GERMANUS OF CONSTANTINOPLE)

8. Today is the prelude to God's munificence and the announcement of the salvation of men. In the temple of God, the Virgin is visible to all, foretelling the coming of Christ. The Virgin, the sacred treasury of God's glory, enters today into the house of the Lord, bringing with her the grace of the divine Spirit. The angels are stunned as they behold the most pure one coming in, and say, "What a wonder is this?" The Virgin enters into the Holy of Holies. O Mother of God,

you are the precious Ark of God, no profane hand may touch you. But the lips of the faithful will never cease to sing your praise, repeating with joy the angels' words, "O pure Virgin, you are indeed raised above all creatures." (NINTH CENTURY, BYZANTINE LITURGY)

9. Today she who will receive the Holy of Holies, that is the Christ, through the sanctification of the Holy Spirit, is, through an even greater sanctification, placed in the Holy of Holies with holiness and majesty. There where only the High Priest may enter, and then rarely, only once a year, it is there in this holy sanctuary of grace that Mary is offered to stay. Who has ever heard anything similar? Who has ever seen or heard, now or formerly, that a woman was introduced into the intimacy of the Holy of Holies, and that it was in this place, almost inaccessible even to men, that she lived and ate. Is this not a striking demonstration of the strange magnificence of which her womb would be the object? Is it not a manifest sign, an irrefutable proof? (ST. GERMANUS OF CONSTANTINOPLE)

10. And Mary was held in admiration by all the people of Israel. When she was three years old she walked with a step so mature and spoke so perfectly that all were astonished. She was so constant in prayer, and her appearance was so beautiful and glorious, that scarcely any one could look into her face. And she occupied herself constantly with her wool-work, so that in her tender years she could do things even grown women are unable to do. And this was the order that she set for herself; from the morning to the third hour to remain in prayer, from the third to the ninth to do her weaving, and

from the ninth, once again, to return herself to prayer. She would not stop her prayers until an angel of the Lord would appear to her, and from his hand she used to receive food. Mary thus became more and more perfect in the work of God. (FOURTH CENTURY, PSEUDO MATTHEW)

GLORY BE TO THE FATHER   Glory be to the Father, and to the Son, and to the Holy Spirit, as it was in the beginning, is now and ever shall be, world without end. Amen.

THE FATIMA PRAYER   O my Jesus, forgive us our sins, save us from the fires of hell, lead all souls to heaven, especially those in most need of Thy mercy.

The Chaste Espousals of Our Lady and Saint Joseph

FRUIT OF THE MYSTERY

A greater esteem for the virtue of chastity and of a life given exclusively to God

HE VIRGIN MARY, BLESSED, holy and pure, was already twelve years old. For her parents offered her in the temple when she was three years of age and she remained in the temple of the Lord nine years. Then, when the priests saw that the virgin, holy and God-fearing, was growing up, they spoke to each other, saying, "Let us search out a man, righteous and pious, to whom Mary may be entrusted until the time of her marriage; lest we sin in keeping a woman in the temple and draw down God's anger." Therefore they immediately sent out, and assembled twelve men of the tribe of Judah. And they wrote down the names of the twelve tribes of Israel. And the lot fell upon the pious old man, righteous Joseph. Then the priests answered, and said to the Blessed Virgin, "Go with Joseph, and be with him till the time of your marriage." Righteous Joseph therefore received her, and led her away to his own house. And after the holy virgin had spent two years in his house her age was exactly fourteen years. (FOURTH CENTURY, THE HISTORY OF JOSEPH THE CARPENTER)

OUR FATHER   Our Father, Who art in Heaven, hallowed be Thy name, Thy kingdom come, Thy will be done, on earth as it is in heaven. Give us this day our daily bread; and forgive us our trespasses, as we forgive those who trespass against us; and lead us not into temptation, but deliver us from evil. Amen.

HAIL MARY (10)   Hail Mary, Full of Grace, the Lord is with thee. Blessed art thou among women and blessed is the fruit of thy womb, Jesus. Holy Mary, Mother of God, pray for us sinners now, and at the hour of our death. Amen.

1. "Joseph was a carpenter by trade, more famous in this craft than all other carpenters, because he was going to be a servant to the true craftsman, the creator and architect of all creatures. But just as Joseph was famous at that time for his trade, so was he also for his virtue, his piety, and his good

works: among those of his age he was the greatest, except for the parents of the Virgin." * (ST. MAXIMUS THE CONFESSOR)

2. The priests sent a herald through all the tribes of Israel, that on the third day all should come together into the temple of the Lord. And when all the people had come together, Abiathar the high priest rose to the highest step and said, "Hear me, O sons of Israel, and receive my words into your ears. Ever since this temple was built by Solomon there have been in it virgins, the daughters of kings, and the daughters of prophets and of priests, and they were great, and worthy of admiration. But when they came to the proper age they were given in marriage, and followed the course of their mothers before them, and were pleasing to God. But a new order of life has been found by Mary alone, who promises that she will remain a virgin to God. Wherefore it seems to me that we should try to ascertain to whose keeping she ought to be entrusted." (FOURTH CENTURY, PSEUDO MATTHEW)

3. The lot was cast by the priests upon the twelve tribes, and the lot fell upon the tribe of Judah. And the high priest said, "Tomorrow let every one who has no wife come, and bring a flower-less branch in his hand. And so it happened that Joseph brought his branch along with the other men. And the rods having been handed over to the high priest, the priest offered a sacrifice to the Lord God, and inquired of the Lord. And the Lord said to him, "Put all their rods into the holy of holies and let them remain there, and order the men to

---

* Maximus the Confessor, *"The Life of the Virgin"*, (Yale: Bloomsbury 2012), 96.

return tomorrow to receive back their branches, and the man from the point of whose rod a dove shall come forth, and fly towards heaven, and in whose hand the rod, when given back, shall exhibit this sign, to him let Mary be delivered to be kept." (FOURTH CENTURY, PSEUDO MATTHEW)

4. The high priest went into the holy of holies and brought forth the rods. And when he had distributed the rods, the dove did not come forth from any of them. Joseph however had not yet collected his, instead he was humbly standing last of all. The high priest cried out to him with a loud voice, saying, "Come, Joseph, and receive your rod; for we are waiting for you." And Joseph came up trembling, because the high priest had called him with a very loud voice. But as soon as he stretched forth his hand, and laid hold of his rod, immediately from the top of it came forth a dove whiter than snow, exceedingly beautiful, which, after long flying about the roofs of the temple, at length flew towards the heavens. Then all the people congratulated the old man, saying, "You have been made blessed in your old age, O father Joseph, seeing that God has shown you to be fit to receive Mary." And the priests said to him, "Take her, because of all the tribe of Judah you alone have been chosen by God." (FOURTH CENTURY, PSEUDO MATTHEW)

5. "The Lord gave an excellent sign, and Joseph's rod blossomed and became fruitful as Aaron's before it, and so by the providence of God and by the deliberation of the priests Joseph received from the Zechariah the Immaculate Virgin as a guardian and her caregiver and a servant of the mystery

that is great and wonderful beyond all comprehension." ** (ST. MAXIMUS THE CONFESSOR)

6. "And Joseph was then more than seventy years old, so that no one could raise any suspicions whatsoever of marriage. And he was poor and lacking in material possessions, so that in his house was raised, according to bodily stature, the one who became poor for our sakes in order to enrich us with his divinity." ** (ST. MAXIMUS THE CONFESSOR)

7. Five virgins accompanied Mary when she left from the temple, and they were given to her for her company until the appointed day of the marriage. And so Joseph received Mary with the other five virgins who were to join her. These virgins were Rebecca, Sephora, Susanna, Abigea, and Cael. The girls took with them different coloured silk, fine linen and flax, and they cast lots among themselves as to which embroidery each of them should do. For Mary it was to make the purple veil of the Holy of Holies. When Mary received this task, the other girls said to her, "Since you are the least, the most humble, and the youngest among us, it is right for you to receive and be allotted this task." (FOURTH CENTURY, PSEUDO MATTHEW)

8. Others may have stated that 'the brethren of the Lord' were the children of Joseph, but I do not see it so. Rather I claim that Joseph himself, on account of Mary, was a virgin. From a virgin wedlock a virgin son was born. Joseph was indeed

---

** Maximus the Confessor, *"The Life of the Virgin"*, (Yale: Bloomsbury 2012), 48.

the guardian of Mary and her true husband. I conclude that he who was thought worthy to be called father of the Lord, remained a virgin. Nor do we say this to condemn marriage, for virginity itself is the fruit of marriage; but because when we are dealing with saints we must not judge rashly. (ST. JEROME)

9. The angel spoke to Joseph without deceit when he said, "Do not fear to take Mary, your wife, to your home." Mary is already called his wife because of the commitment of betrothal. Because of their fidelity to this union, they are both deservedly called 'parents' of Christ even though only Mary was His mother according to the flesh. The entire good of the nuptial institution was present in the case of their marriage: there was offspring, there was faithfulness, there was the bond. As offspring, we recognise the Lord Jesus Himself; the fidelity, in that there was no infidelity; the bond, because there was no separation. (ST. AUGUSTINE)

10. And so the Lord came by an espoused virgin, in order to elude the notice of the wicked one, for being espoused she was pledged to be her husband's. Hear what the prophet Isaiah says about this man and the Virgin, "The book that is sealed shall be delivered to a man that is learned." What is meant by this sealed book, but the Virgin undefiled? From whom is this to be given? From the priests evidently. And to whom? To the artisan Joseph. The priests espoused Mary to Joseph as to a prudent husband, and committed her to his care in expectation of the time of marriage. "The book that is sealed shall be delivered to a man that is learned." But that man will say, "I cannot read it." But why can't you read it, O Joseph? "I cannot read it," he says, "because the book is

sealed." For whom, then, is it preserved? It is preserved as a place of sojourn for the Maker of the universe. (ST. GREGORY THAUMATURGUS)

GLORY BE TO THE FATHER   Glory be to the Father, and to the Son, and to the Holy Spirit, as it was in the beginning, is now and ever shall be, world without end. Amen.

THE FATIMA PRAYER   O my Jesus, forgive us our sins, save us from the fires of hell, lead all souls to heaven, especially those in most need of Thy mercy.

CONCLUDING PRAYERS   *Upon completing the recitation of the Holy Rosary, the following prayers are customary, but others too may be added according to one's devotion and preference.*

HAIL HOLY QUEEN PRAYER   Hail Holy Queen, Mother of Mercy, hail our life, our sweetness and our hope. To thee do we cry, poor banished children of Eve, to thee do we send up our sighs, mourning and weeping in this vale of tears. Turn then, most gracious advocate, thine eyes of mercy towards us, and after this, our exile, show unto us the blessed fruit of thy womb, Jesus. O clement, O loving, O sweet Virgin Mary. Pray for us O holy Mother of God, that we may be made worthy of the promises of Christ.

Let Us Pray   O God, Whose only begotten son, by His life, death and resurrection, has purchased for us the rewards of eternal life, grant we beseech Thee, that meditating on these mysteries of the most Holy Rosary of the Blessed Virgin Mary, we may both imitate what they contain and obtain what they promise, through the same Christ our Lord. Amen.

SAINT MICHAEL THE ARCHANGEL PRAYER   Holy Michael, the Archangel, defend us in the day of battle. Be our safeguard against the wickedness and snares of the devil. May God rebuke him, we humbly pray; and do thou, O Prince of the heavenly hosts, by the power of God thrust down into hell Satan and all the evil spirits who wander through the world seeking the ruin of souls. Amen.

MEMORARE PRAYER   Remember, O most gracious Virgin Mary, that never was it known that anyone who fled to thy protection, implored thy help, or sought thine intercession was left unaided. Inspired by this confidence, I fly unto thee, O Virgin of virgins, my mother; to thee do I come, before thee I stand, sinful and sorrowful. O Mother of the Word Incarnate, despise not my petitions, but in thy mercy hear and answer me. Amen.

May the Divine Assistance remain always with us, and may the souls of the faithful departed, through the mercy of God rest in peace. Amen.

Made in the USA
Las Vegas, NV
17 February 2021

17899976R00111